# The Memory Bird

The three editors of this anthology all work within help
groups for abused survivors.

Linda Farthing is a trained social worker and
therapist. She has over ten years experience of
working with adults and children who are trying to
overcome the effects of sexual abuse.

Caroline Malone works for Open University. She
has also worked with self-help groups for over five
years. She is married and has two sons.

Lorraine Marce lectures and conducts research in the
areas of social psychology and child sexual abuse.
She has been active in the survivor movement
and in the promotion of the rights of children
and young people in the law.

# The Memory Bird

## Survivors of Sexual Abuse

It followed me around like a bad smell
Like the stone I couldn't find in my shoe
That memory bird, who whispered in
my ear - now I thank her, for telling me

JANINE GUICE

EDITED BY

*Caroline Malone, Linda Farthing, and Lorraine Marce*

T Temple University Press

Temple University Press, Philadelphia 19122
Published 1997

First published in Great Britain by Virago Press 1996

Printed in the United States of America

⊗ The paper used in this publication meets the requirements of the
American National Standard for Information Sciences—Permanence of
Paper for Printed Library Materials, ANSI Z39.48–1984

Text design by Eliz. Anne O'Donnell

Cataloging-in-Publication Data available from the Library of Congress

ISBN 1-56639-525-9 cloth
ISBN 1-56639-526-7 paper

# Contents

# Acknowledgments

We would like to thank the following people who played a major part in the creation of this anthology:

Lindsay, who was in the original group who brought the idea to life and has continued to be part of the editorial process.

Ray Wilmott, who has also contributed to the editorial process throughout.

Jan Walmsley, who gave us the benefit of her professional expertise as editor of an anthology and a writer.

After the first selection we asked a group of people to act as critical readers and to give us their input. This was a vital part of the process and helped to ensure that the widest possible range of views is represented in the anthology. We would like to thank them for their help—Charis Alland, Caroline Archer, Gill de la Cour, Penny Hosking, Jean Lancashire, Paula Leach, Penny Kay, Lindsay, Wendy Louise Stern, Ron Wiener, Steve Williams and Ray Wilmott. We drew together the critical readers from those who attended a workshop we held in March 1994 which played a very important role in shaping the anthology. We would like to thank all those who attended the workshop which included all the critical readers and also Richie Butler, Ann Dartnall, Athena Pite, Kim Etherington, Kirstin McDowell, Jo Cottee, Heather McEwan-Lennox, Beth Follini, Hilda Rapp and Linda Hyland. Many of those who attended contributed work to the anthology. Jo, Kirstin and Athena also represented the newsletter *Fighting Back*, which gave us a great deal of support and helped us to contact many of our contributors.

We would like to thank Becky Swift and Melanie Silgardo, formerly of Virago, for their belief in us and their encouragement, Professor Malcolm Johnson who as Dean of the School of Health and Social Welfare at the Open University, where Caroline works, gave this project his full support and Antonet Roberts, who patiently typed the handwritten entries and handled many phone enquiries with discretion and sensitivity.

We would like to acknowledge all those who wrote to us, offering their support and encouragement and sent us material. We were not able to use pieces from everyone nor to use all the pieces any individual sent, but the wider picture that we gained from reading through all the material and the letters and from the phone conversations was the key to building the final shape of the anthology. We have tried to ensure that all the voices we heard are represented in the work we have finally selected.

# Introduction

This anthology has been co-operatively written and produced by a number of women and men who have experienced sexual abuse in childhood: it portrays and unravels some of the many layers of our lives as survivors of these experiences. As a result, the book is inevitably many things at once: it is a tribute to our collective strengths; it recognizes our differences; it is a signal of the pain we continue to suffer; it is about our spirit and our spirituality; it speaks of our healing—and lack of it; it documents our relationships; it unchains our collective voices on our own terms through diary extracts, poetry, prose, letters and artwork.

As survivors we demand to be taken seriously for who and what we are, and not for what others assume us to be. For too long, survivors of child sexual abuse have been at the receiving end of knowledge. Much of this knowledge has been produced through the practices and beliefs of a number of "experts" or "professionals" who are not survivors themselves. We tend to be described by knowledge produced by these experts as being damaged and damaging citizens; citizens who are frequently seen as the flawed by-products of abusive relationships; damaged citizens who need to be described, examined, quantified, understood and ultimately controlled—for our own good. Survivors who become experts, practitioners or professionals in the field are often placed in a position where they cannot openly acknowledge what has happened to them in the past, as this might damage their job and career prospects. This is another way in which we are denied a way of talking about our experiences in our own terms in a society that eagerly awaits the next "child sexual abuse scandal," but remains silent about the ways in which the children of these scandals (and those who do not make it to the headlines) are stigmatized in adulthood.

The silence, secrecy and shame that still besieges the whole area of child sexual abuse all too often results in the fact that we are afforded limited opportunities to hear each other's voices, to give and receive support, and to challenge much of the negativity that prevents us from talking about and living our lives in ways that are more complete. While we may struggle to come to terms with abuse in various ways, and may need help in order to do so, surviving is not all we do, and survivors is not all we are. We are, and do, many things, as this book will hopefully show.

Nadia, in her letter to us, makes this point eloquently:

> **I am an incest survivor and have been having counselling for about five months but that is not all I am. I wanted to write this story to show the great strength and hope survivors have. . . . I live in the inner city of Sydney and am a practicing artist, I am also involved with a women's performance group and do meditation and yoga.**

It is only by reclaiming and owning *all* of our experiences at every level, whoever we are and wherever we are, and by presenting these with our own voices and in our own terms, that we will begin to be taken seriously. We see this book as an important step in this struggle.

## Why the Memory Bird?

The title for the anthology was inspired by a design by Janine Guice. It encapsulates the idea that healing comes from within ourselves and that the way our memories work is both a protection and a way of holding the truth until we can use it. They also capture one of the ways in which childhood experiences haunt adult life. "The Memory Bird" is a symbol of our multiple and personal truths.

## How we produced the anthology

From the outset we decided that the anthology must include contributions from, and represent the voices of, survivors from as wide a range of backgrounds as possible, which inevitably involved cutting across gender, age, class, sexuality, ethnic and regional boundaries. In order to achieve this diversity, we sent information about the anthology to a number of settings (for example to medical practices, Well Woman clinics, theaters, cinemas, network television, community and university bulletin boards), and via informal as well as formal survivor networks in the U.K., Australia and Canada. Additionally, we adopted a number of strategies to ensure that we dealt as sensitively as we could with the material that we received. One such strategy was to hold a meeting in London, to which a number of survivors from all over the country who had responded to our early calls for contributions were invited. At this meeting we worked through our own ideas for the anthology and received many helpful suggestions from those who took the time to make the journey to London and those who sent us suggestions in the mail. The time and assistance offered by many of those who attended the initial meeting continued throughout the development of this book. Forming a wider editorial and critical reading group, they offered us direction and feedback, they supported us throughout the process of material selection and editing, and shared the sheer hard work that is involved in the final stages of preparing a book. Without their help we feel that we could not have met our aspirations.

## The structure of the book

In pulling the various contributions together, we were faced with a number of dilemmas. One major dilemma related to the organization of the diverse material. After exploring numerous formats, we decided to present it in a way that reflected a number of the recurring themes or motifs we had identified. These themes, which include belonging, remembering, survival, transitions and pain, were then placed into chapters. We named the chapters by using extracts from the contributions themselves, like "Can You Hear Me?" or "Learning to Dance": in so doing, we captured the essential qualities and character of the chapter in the terms used by the authors.

The chapters then had to follow some kind of sequence, which gave rise to another dilemma: the tyranny of order. In choosing a particular order we did not want to imply that there are linear pathways, stages or processes through which we have passed, or will pass. Such approaches, we feel, do little justice to the layered complexity of our lives: what we have in common as well as our differences, and the varied ways in which we choose to convey these complexities, similarities and differences. Instead we hope that you will see the anthology as a series of overlapping and interconnected observations and commentaries about ourselves and our lives.

We begin each chapter with a short introduction that gives a feel for the range of material that is included as well as highlighting a small sample of pieces that speak to the particular theme being addressed. We have tried to keep these introductions succinct in order to make room for as many contributions as possible. In each case, we refer to the authors in the way that they wished to be known.

# The Memory Bird

# The blades of my life

"The blades of my life" is an exploration of pain. The pain that many of us struggle to live with is an important place to start the anthology and from which to move on. The chapter mainly consists of poetry, as this appeared to be an immediate and accessible vehicle that could best express the raw emotions that are part of pain: feelings of rage, despair, loss, grief, hopelessness, desperation and being alone. This chapter may be difficult for some to read, as there is very little reference to the positive side of these stark emotions.

Penny K., in "A diary of feelings," describes the pain involved in an activity which many may take for granted. Penny describes waking up as being "unable to move and scared by the thought of the day ahead and being alive." The authors of "I smack shit out of walls," "The blades of my life" and "Alert" each reflect the different ways in which they externalize the pain.

The anonymous contribution entitled "Thoughts of a lady" documents the ways in which the author was held accountable by her mother for the abuse that occurred. Here she describes the pain that is bound up in a sense of worthlessness, the constant struggle against feelings of inferiority, and the fear of people that ensued.

Finally, many of the authors highlighted the agonizing and tormenting relationship between life and death within a context of living with the pain. Brenda Nicklinson's piece "Indirect murder" and Vicki Strickland's diary extract both deal with this relationship in very direct terms.

———————

Screaming trapped through the years
Reverberating through the structure
of everyday things
Distending and tearing the fabric
of domestic tranquillity
Damming the flowing energy
Creating stagnant pools and uncontrollable floods.
Choking in my throat. Tension singing in my tendons,
Freed only through the present release
of the old pain—
But would the scream stop, once released?

CAROLINE MALONE

## Scared to show my true colors

Multi-talented, they say
As if advertising me
On special offer
While stocks last.
A little bit here
A little bit there
Is what I show.
A glimpse
Of my feathers.
Show too much and they'll tear you apart
Bird of Paradise
Born in the trenches
Facing the mouth of a gun.

EMILY BIRD

## Unaffected moment

There's an unaffected moment,
That waits at my window,
And if I'm feeling lonely
I'll go there, for someone to talk to.

For there's something vaguely precious,
In its silent thoughtfulness,
And its welcoming warmth,
That I won't realize that the day has gone.
                              I'll just feel better.

RAE-SARAH HOUSE

## I see too much

I look on, I see no future
I look on still, see no peace,
I sense sadness, too much anguish
I'm looking on in disbelief,
I look on, I see no smiling
I look on still, true love has gone,
I sense the air, there is no laughter
the bird has lost his springtime song,
I look on, I see no sharing
I look on still I see no hope
I sense that mother earth is screaming
life is still one nasty joke.
I look on I see no exit
I look on still, can't take no more
I sense that things could not be harder
I've closed my eyes, my only door.

SELINA NICHOLAS

## A diary of feelings

As I wake up I am aware of feeling distant and fuzzy. It takes me a while to focus on the room around me and what is happening. Waking is the worst part of the day at the moment—slowly coming out of the reality of my dreams and trying to focus on the present. This morning I am left with a bitter taste of fear and anger, and images of being chased and attacked. I feel heavy and weighed down, unable to move and scared by the thought of the day ahead and being alive.

It is at moments like this that I know that I have to look after myself and help myself feel better—I'm the only person here, I guess! I try to tell myself that everything's ok, and to let go of the feelings and memories I have woken with. I get out of bed, still feel sick and a bit shaky. I have got a slight cold this morning, which always makes me feel strangely spaced out and reminds me of floating away during the abuse. Sometimes I feel so frustrated that so much in everyday life can trigger me back to those times.

I open the curtains and realize that it is a beautiful sunny day. I love the sun and immediately I begin to feel better—energized by the warmth and color of its rays. I breathe more deeply and feel calmer and grounded. I sit and let my thoughts wander for a while and then contemplate reading a book. As usual I have bought another book about sexual abuse to read. I feel this is almost a compulsion of mine—a desperation to feel connected with other survivors and to try to gain as much understanding as possible about my own experiences. Yet I am not sure that reading these books always helps me, as I can become lost in my own and others' pain. This morning I flick through the book, but manage to listen to a voice inside me saying I am not feeling strong enough to face the abuse head on today. I leave the book and go and eat crumpets for breakfast instead—yum!

I run my bath feeling quite content and happy. I light a candle and the sunlight comes in through the window. I find it hard to look at my body in daylight, and as I undress I wish that it would disappear. I try to ignore it and quickly get into the water, submerging myself under lots of bubbles. The water is warm and soothing, and I lie there drifting off into my own thoughts. I begin to think about all the people I met at the survivors' workshop on Saturday, and suddenly I feel so full of sadness and anger for all the abuse that happens in the world. I start to cry, and for a few minutes feel total despair and a wish to be dead. But then the feelings lift as I make myself breathe and I feel I can cope again. The anger within me feels strong and healing, and I climb out of the bath as a powerful woman!

For the next few hours my moods keep alternating. I sit in the sun in the lounge and feel peaceful and calm. Thoughts about abuse seem a long way away, and for a while I am kept busy trying to disconnect my car radio so it can be repaired. Amazingly I actually manage to achieve this without any major disasters to myself or the radio, and I feel proud of myself. I am not the most practical of people!

In the afternoon I walk from my flat into town to go shopping. It is a nice walk, through the tree-lined streets where I live. I feel safe in my neighborhood, having moved six months ago to a place where my family can no longer find me, and I enjoy feeling alive walking in the sun and the cold. However, as I wander round town doing odds and ends my mood suddenly changes and I begin to feel heavy and depressed. I am angry about this—nothing major has happened to upset me, but a number of small things seem so easily to trigger the pain I have inside me. Sometimes I feel totally out of control, as if the feelings have a life of their own regardless of my efforts to heal. The hardest thing for me today is seeing people from my past in the distance and not feeling able to go and say hello to them. A few years ago, before I began facing up to my feelings and telling people the truth about my past, I could easily have talked to anyone and pretended that everything was ok. But now that I have let go of the façade I used to put on I can no longer pretend so easily, and I have found that most people do not want to know me while I am acknowledging the abuse I am healing from. It feels very lonely and empty, and sometimes I wish I could go back to a time before the return of memories and expression of feelings.

As I feel more depressed I find myself drawn towards the supermarket and end up buying myself lots of nice food for tea. Now that I have no job and am living on benefit this is something that I cannot really afford to do, but sometimes it is the only thing that can help me feel better. Luckily I never seem to put on weight! I go home and spend hours sitting watching rubbish tv and eating. Slowly, and with relief, I feel the heaviness lift and my mind becomes occupied with what I am watching. It is evening and I feel peaceful watching the sunset and listening to the birds singing outside my window.

As the evening wears on and it begins to get dark I feel more heavy and tired. I find I get tired so easily these days and I hate it. I become very aware of the quiet and being alone. After a whole day by myself this time of night is very difficult for me.

Later a counselor from Rape Crisis whom I talk to rings me up. It is wonderful to hear her voice after the silence and to be offered some support. However, after having been alone all day I find that the words and feelings are frozen within me and it takes time for them to thaw. I gradually manage to speak, although I still cannot cry, and I feel over-whelmed with feelings of sadness and anger towards my father.

After an hour Jenny goes and I am left by myself again. I lie in bed in the dark, scared by the shadows around me and finding it hard not to panic. I take some herbal sleeping tablets in the hope that I can sleep and try to clear my mind and relax. It takes a few hours for the thoughts and feelings to subside and eventually I fall asleep and another night of dreams begins.

PENNY K.

## An introduction

Sitting alone
In a group of people;
I know;
They don't;
I know they don't know

Though, sometimes
I suspect
They suspect
That they know something
About me
Which smells.
Which is why I smile
And exude friendliness
To mask the smell.

Sometimes I hug,
So as to be hugged,
Comforted,
Childlike
To receive
Never
Yet
Brutally thrust
Given
But it's never ever
Never never
Can't—couldn't be
Enough
Love
To fill
My abused, gaping, empty, buggered hole,
Unfilled
For ever and ever
Amen.

RON WIENER

## Diary extract

I have, on and off, kept a "diary." That is, odd pieces of paper which I wrote on when desperate or depressed, and I have kept them. The themes which run through the past fifteen years of writing are summed up in a piece I wrote when I took some time out from my relationship about six years ago, to try and think about why I felt so bad so much of the time:

> I can't cope with my feelings of confusion—what I feel about me and what others say—they're so different. I just want to escape. I just want to go, to live alone. I want somebody to help me. I want to run away from my relationship. Why? It's not just *me*! Is it? I depend on my partner too much. Do I? I keep wanting to walk out. So that's a problem. Why do I think he's a fuckin' pig? Is it because I'm angry with myself? It's difficult to understand how much of a pain I am. I feel so guilty, so ashamed. Of what? Am I really so pathetic and despicable? Why do I feel so sorry for myself? I feel like writing: Dear Jack I am fucked up and freaked out. The problems of a difficult upbringing? Inadequate? Pathetic? Whatever, this is me now and I can't handle you or me or at least not together. So—goodbye is what I want to say. And then what? Do what? Run away to what? I'm no good. I can't be that bad, can I? Everything is my fault, I feel ashamed and guilty and don't know why. I'm a reasonably intelligent woman. I can't see a solution.
>
> There's been a ghastly mistake. I can't bear the contradictions. I don't want to spend the rest of my life like this.

ANGIE KELLY

---

Screw you man, why do you have to keep haunting me? I mean as if it's not enough that you've ruined the first part of my life and I'm now trying to overcome that you have to keep invading my dreams and scare me half shitless in flashbacks.

What is it that makes it ok for you to do this to children?

SARAH

## My brother

The "abuse" I suffered at four (from my older brother) continued on and off for around fourteen years or so—when there were attempts to force me into oral and anal sex, though these attempts were not successful.

The most telling devastation really was to do with the manner of his continuous "assumptions" bordering on a kind of brainwashing technique which was nothing more than a non-stop mockery of myself as being trouble-making, attempts at making me seem and feel stupid, taking in the frequent introduction to strangers (to me) who would then proceed to tell me that they'd heard what a "nasty person" I am, while he'd be smirking in the background. Along similar lines was the fact that when visited by relatives from abroad—who having meanwhile *first* visited my brother (and unknown to me would be "advised," as to the "kind" of person I am) would visit myself and my family—as part of a good idea thought up by my brother—and the first "awkward moments" would be not so much to do with natural shyness, but a secret and collusive sniggering campaign going on between the visitors and my brother—"a secret joke"?—and all the time my brother would occupy a stance that suggested that he, and only he, is the moving force behind all the arrangements, even to the extent of taking the credit, and receiving thanks, which were rightly due to us, for all the hard work behind our usually extremely generous hospitality.

The fact that I did not twig what was going on, is due entirely to his endless onslaught on my personality and reputation . . .

While watching a U.K. documentary on "Child sexual abuse within the family" I "discovered" all the poison and lies and filthy deceits—my eyes were opened and I cried for weeks. The mere thought of the idea that what happened *happened to me*, and that *all the guilt and shame was his, his, totally his*.

In those moments I was so very relieved, so very, very *released*, and every dirty little trick that my brother had perpetrated on me was now so very crystal clear—*how could I have been so very stupid*—Now I could see how deeply ashamed I had become, and in such a self-depreciating way that nothing was bad enough, that happened, it was as if I needed the most dreadful things to happen to me, as if I really deserved it, and as if I would become better by suffering these things, like a kind of emotional and spiritual flagellation.

And then the *anger*.

This has been almost life-threatening. Things such as raised blood pressure, massive nose-bleeds, crippling headaches, and periods of real teeth-grinding rage, when the tension is like being in a steel strait-jacket . . . this morning I visited my doctor and was told to "calm down"—this person just does not, and cannot, understand. It wasn't to do with my brother Frank—he died two years ago. No, I realize that I have managed to choose people in my life that have a relationship to the kinds of experiences I've undergone, and so repeat the abuse—over and over—again and again . . .

JOHN STREETIN

JOHN STREETIN

## The blades of my life

Flesh wounds
Near death wounds, unseen
Heart burned
Lesson learned
Missing a scream
Deep cuts, just visible cuts
Big cuts for the slut
Kind days, sublime days
Feeling so uncared

So disturbed
Never mind, worries over
I have found
My four leaved clover
In dirty sand so mixed with oil
In the summer on my lawn
In the place the frog spawned
Night, night, little wonder
Bye, bye, farewell
Look in the mirror, ponder
See my eyes stare back and yell
I want to go to bed
I'm tired, a long life
Let me rest my head
A while on a sharp knife

HEATHER MCEWAN-LENNOX

## Recognition

They call it
Somatization disorder

A technical term for
"it's all in the mind, dear"

No cancer, only

Numerous physical symptoms
Throughout my pain-ridden body

Whose crude language speaks
For my despair

As years ago I feared
The terror and betrayal
Of the night

But depression has frozen
Both memory and emotion

And cancer serves as a metaphor
A symbolic representation
Of the past

A means of expressing
The otherwise inexpressible

As the body remembers what
My mind cannot face

ALEX BENJAMIN


## A child remembers Christmas dinner

Christmas was coming,
the goose had got too fat.
Daddy stuffed it quickly hiding
feathers in his hat.

Mummy roasted baby bird,
and carved her milk-white breast.
Then they snapped my sacred bone
and told me I was blessed.

RUNA WOLF

## The dark companion

Treacherous and seemingly hazardous are the paths to life. Distant, almost in another era lay the happy memories, encased within a dark and perilous zone. For surging through my veins are the uncertainties and cruelties of my day-to-day existence. Crashing with incredible ferocity against my inner will to survive. Corroding away at my resistance peeling away my defenses, leaving me easy prey for manipulation and vulnerable to anyone.

The fears that ravish within run rampant, infesting anything in their path. A mounting, a seething mass of fear forcing me to become subservient, confused, and ever closer to submitting to the powers that be. To just stand and watch as the avalanche of emotions fight for the right to rule.

A constant companion is the inexorable darkness, one I know I can depend on to be ever present regardless. My friend! Yet, an enemy greatly feared for its strength and will to control.

ANN MACPHERSON

## Extract from a diary

*15 October 1987*
A day off school—car broke down the night before and a day off was due. In a hole again—my brain is good at digging these.

All the heart-wrenching, soul-searching is fine—but what does it solve? 11.30 a.m. Thursday morning and I still feel dreadful—I haven't done a thing. I've self-indulged in a book, in my self-indulgent "verse"; self-indulged in food and now I'm self-indulging in guilt.

*1988* I want to SCREAM.

4 July 1992 Suicide: That black Tuesday
I want to die
And did in a way.

*18 June 1993* **Feelings**
Bus late. Raining hard.
Feel tired and low so buy and eat chewing nuts,
Get home and nobody there. So eat toast,
crumpet, apple, orange, yogurt. Feel full.
Felt alone.

*2 July 1993* 28 years old, nearly 29
This is the blackest phase of my life ever.
    Nearly trained as a psychiatric nurse, nearly completed my MA dissertation and I have come crashing down. My innards have stirred and stormed; struggling and want out; drowning and wanting to drown, just let go.

VICKI STRICKLAND

(*Vicki was sexually abused by a schoolteacher*)


## Indirect murder

> When all is said and done,
> as if it ever could be,
> the issue of suicide is not one
> that rates much sympathy.
>
> Murder, for some reason, is more
> written about and understood.
> To the box office, glorified gore
> is artistically valid and good.

Murderers and murdered are news. Fame
or even notoriety is their lot.
Suicide is looked upon with shame
as something it's better we all forgot.

Yet suicide is murder in disguise,
caused by some unremembered crime,
not understood by our present eyes,
for it has its roots in an earlier time.

Because we don't know the beginning
of such long-term murder, we see
suicides as people who are sinning
and reject them accordingly.

Those untouched by such murder, in resentment
or fear, not knowing enough about
it, come up with some facile comment
such as "Suicide is the coward's way out."

Like primitive man, who saw
no relation between sex and birth,
and later man, whose immature and raw
greed fatally threatens the earth,

we seem totally unable to relate
effect to a cause that isn't obvious to see
or to realize that a suicide's state
is murder rooted in personal history.

Not by something as obvious as a knife
or a gun, but by acts that the perpetrator
cannot recognize as threatening to life
because the dying happens years later.

BRENDA NICKLINSON

## Alert

Since I was hurt
I've lived alert
Never sleeping
Always peeping
Constant strain
Muscle pain.

Now release
Will give me peace.

ANGIE

## In my temper

Once when I got in a temper
I wrecked a room
First I picked up an armchair
High over my head and threw it hard against the wall
I kicked two panes of glass out of a door
Battered shit out of the walls
Head-butted walls and windows
Punched everything that was solid
But I felt no pain
I had lots of energy and I had to stem my temper
I picked up a piece of glass and cut my arms
I wanted to feel something
To let me know I was alive
To let these around me know I was alive
They already knew but I just felt dead
I couldn't control what I did
When the staff tried to stop me
I kicked them, punched them, butted them

And then carried on smacking shit out of the wall
Then someone grabbed my arms
Then all I could do was kick
Kick and scream and swear
Someone held me tight to them
I started to calm down a bit
But I was scared
And I still felt numb
I didn't even feel the pain I should have
From my cut arms
Then I was put on one to one
Not allowed to go anywhere without staff
Not the bedroom, or bathroom or toilet
So I didn't
I died again

"CARLA"

## Thoughts of a lady

*Thoughts of a lady who was abused by her father until the age of about seven, when she told her mother. He went to prison. The rest of her childhood was terrible: her mother blaming her for what had happened, and for the subsequent poverty.*

Missing out my education. Having no childhood. Was not allowed to play out. Was always having to stay in doing housework. Looking after my younger brothers. Making their bottles for feeds. Getting up in the night when they were teething. Changing their nappies. Feeding them.

Having to go to work, then come home and cook meals for everyone—then do washing and ironing, etc. Never being able to go out when I wanted to.

Being called dirty names. My mum's terrible looks that she would give me as though I was disgusting in some way.

Going to school and worrying about not having any money. I would sit in class trying to work out how much money she would be getting—family allowance, etc.—and then working out what she had to buy—bread, coal—worrying about what she would have left over until she next got some more.

Having to borrow money all the time. She would send me round all the neighbors to ask for money.

The shame I would feel when she and my dad would be fighting in the middle of the morning, and I was forever having to go up the police station for help. Everyone always talking about us.

Her coming to my place of work at lunchtimes and hitting me in front of people I worked with when I was out for lunch. Screaming at me and telling them I was no good.

The nightmares I have. The way I feel about myself.

Being afraid of people.

Not being able to have nice clothes and having sometimes to borrow from a neighbor's daughter something to wear, then her daughter ridiculing me about it.

One time I had to do gym in knickers that had holes in—everyone was laughing at me—I just wanted to die. The teacher didn't do anything about everyone making fun of me. I had to carry on. The teachers all thought I was stupid because I could never do the work.

My marriage not working out.

Not being able to sort out my feelings about how I really do feel about my husband.

Feeling inferior to most people and the struggle that I have trying to not feel that way. The constant struggle gets me down; I never seem to win as hard as I try.

That my brothers and sisters are all screwed up because of their upbringing. I can remember getting a hug off my mum, because it was the only one I got off her. Just once. I was never loved by her in any way. I hate her and yet I love her, too. I feel sorry for her. I feel even now as though she haunts me. I feel as though I carry her on my shoulders all the time, even though I haven't seen or spoken to her for ten years. I feel like that about my husband. He blames me as well because things are not right. He was always find-

ing fault with me, and I do my best for the most part. I can't be all
the things that he wants. I try so hard.

ANN PERRY

———————

I am a woman too full of grief, too full,
I am a woman steeped in sorrow.
My grief is great, my sorrow heavy, and sometimes I must go
          apart from you,
And apart from everyone, and weep.
Go apart and wring my hands,
Go apart and rip my breast, tear my tears out by their roots,
          howl my anguish,
and then sit for hours in silence, in a grief too deep for sound.
Sit apart in a silence like a poisoned wound,
In a silence throbbing like infected flesh,
A silence weighing on my silenced heart,
Sit apart and stare blind at stars, look in death's eye and see
          the length of silence still to come
And I have a longing for the desert where the silences and
          emptiness are greater than my own.

LIZZY COTTRELL

———————————

Walk in cold dear boy
and state your love.
I am here for the taking
all hands fit my glove.
Yet you walk in a hurry
and push me away,
You look at my body
and have nothing to say.

JANINE GUICE

My heart stops to study
the face and the eyes,
It has one sense of yearning
which your frame denies.

I cry to this cold man
my love burning through—
"You mentally undress me
but is that all you will do?"

ANGELA BROWN
(*Written aged fourteen/fifteen*)

JANINE GUICE

you strip me naked to my bones
they are bleached white
one by one feelings are
wrenched from flesh and tossed aside
lost to wither in the heat of anger
or perish in the chilling cold
my soul you pick bare
crushing and twisting my identity
until I no longer recognize
who I am

BERNIE

JANINE GUICE

---

My face is flushed
by the slap
I imagine
to swipe across your face

my tongue is swollen
by the words I have
to spit yours down with

my body is testy
with the might of an anger
which would burn you away

I would crush your perfect act
and you down to your real
sad size
and I'd take your
secrets
and expose the lot
in front of your own audience
and I'd commentate

JANINE GUICE

---

We, the family of the abused,

stand recognizing the dead, and our brothers and sisters,
but not knowing why.
you abused
betrayed
overwhelmed

caged
crushed,
but not destroyed,
give me your voice to scream out hate
& screaming, climb the tower of sorrow,
burning, let me leap
and leaping let me burn
and burning let me know
and knowing
Set me free

LIZZY COTTRELL

## Told how to grow

Sat in a case conference
my future predicted—
growing up too quickly
my childhood restricted.
Losing within me
the person I was,
unnatural lifestyle
unnatural love.
Gladly forgetting
days which had gone,
always those same words
always so wrong.
Turning my cheek
for I'm one on my own
it's all right, I don't mind
it's all I have known.

SELINA NICHOLAS

## I smack shit out of walls

When I smack shit out of walls
It's good, I feel pain
Pain that I can see
Bruises on my hands
I like to feel pain
Because it tells me I'm alive
Sometimes my whole body shakes
I get so angry
But nobody sees it
So I keep on pushing it down
Inside me
Sometimes I get so angry
I don't feel safe
I feel I could smack shit out of someone
So I smack shit out of walls
I'm not safe when I'm angry

"CARLA"

## The man in black

Daddy, please don't send me
to that dark place again:
where I am the pale girl
and the spider is in my hair;
where Mummy is cold in the kitchen,
and I am blinded
by the black and frozen stare.

Daddy, you too gently touch my back,
and soft is the hand that silences,
that stays to numb my mind.

You cannot be warm, for then
how is my head so cold
and my body sick?

H.

## To my oldest brother

Why when I was only eight and still an innocent child, did you decide to abuse me? Did you never ever stop and think just what you were doing to me? Did you never consider how I felt about what you were doing to me? Did my cries and screams not get through to you? I always asked you to stop. I didn't want you touching me. I hated you using my body, as if I wasn't there!

I cried and cried for you to stop, but it was a hopeless plea. You were so much stronger than me and though I tried to get away it was never to be.

I got married when I was eighteen, but it only lasted six months. I was pregnant by the time I left him. Even you didn't believe he had hit me; after all, he was your best friend. I had a girl and for the past ten years I have brought her up on my own, without any help from the family.

It has seemed to me that now I am older you have tried to make up to me for what you did, by giving me money and buying things for my daughter. It is only now I realize this may have been your way of relieving your conscience. No matter what you do, I will never ever forgive you for what you put me through. Abusing me and causing me so much pain and misery that my life never felt like mine. I hate you so much for putting me through all you did. I'll hate you for ever. Now it's your turn to lose. I no longer want you in my life and you do not have the right to see either me, or your niece. I won't let you control my life any more. I am now in control of myself. You cannot hurt me any more.

JOAN MARY SIMPSON

# Sarcoid 10 o'clock

Sentinel fever
tick tock
taps my shoulder
stroke of the clock.
Says it's time
to remind me
of the frailty:
damn fever flash,
I tear off my clothes
as sweat winds
all in discoveries
I didn't know I had,
a tropic drench,
on the dot.
Just to rewarn
of my frailty.
Those limits
are now waiting
in a shadow always
for my overstep,
and the sentinel,
good sentinel,
warning me,
watching them,
watching time.

JULIA BRIDGE

JANINE GUICE

## Why am I afraid to tell you who I am

Repressed emotions may find their outlet in the "acting out" of headaches, skin rashes, allergies, asthma, common colds, aching backs or limbs, but they can also be acted out in the tension of tightened muscles, the slamming of doors, the clenching of fists, the rise of blood pressure, the grinding of teeth, tears, temper tantrums, acts of violence.

We do not bury emotions *dead;* they remain *alive* in our subconscious minds and intestines, to hurt and trouble us.

It is not only much more conducive to an authentic relationship to report our true feelings, but it is equally essential to our integrity and health.

JOHN POWELL

# The survivor's song

This chapter is about belonging and relationships. Many of the pieces emphasize the notion that belonging is as much about feeling excluded, being and feeling alone as it is feeling part of something. Belonging is a crucial aspect of the relationships that we have, that we hope to have, that we have had, and those we attempt to maintain. Many of the pieces we have included here struggle with the ways in which the sense of belonging and relationships are knotted together with communication, trust, self and sexuality.

In her contribution, which provides the title of this chapter, Gill Carter highlights the need for understanding and support from a partner. Ron's contribution describes a range of "Sexual fears" with which we are sure many will be able to identify on some level, but which few are given the opportunity to openly acknowledge and explore.

In "The long-term effects of incestuous child sexual abuse" Caroline explores another aspect of belonging and relationships, this time through the experience of parenting. Caroline's account is of the rational action she took to avoid replaying her own childhood experiences with her son, striving to create a stable and nurturing environment for him, and growing in the process.

## The long-term effects of incestuous
## child sexual abuse

If the patterns of childrearing were entirely formed by the parent's own direct experiences then the human race would probably have died out several thousand years ago. Fortunately we do have the ability to learn from other sources than our immediate family and to change the pattern of severely dysfunctional families, such as those in which the emotional, sexual and/or physical abuse of children occurs. People whose own childhood experiences were traumatic can provide good parenting for their own children, despite the damaging myths about survivors becoming abusers of their own children or marrying abusers and failing to protect their children. Both happen, but not on the scale suggested by the media. If even 10 per cent became abusers then pedophilia would have become the sexual norm in our society by now, given that there is evidence that child sexual abuse has occurred in nearly every known civilization. In fact most children grow up to become responsible and caring parents who struggle very hard indeed to overcome the pain and the difficulties caused by events in their own childhoods.

Bringing up children when your own childhood has left wounds which are often unhealed well into adulthood is hard, and I wanted to share some of the difficulties that I have myself experienced and that I have heard other women talk and write about in newsletters, personal accounts, self-help groups and private conversations. I was abused by my father and have spent many years healing from the wounds of this secret and deeply shameful form of child abuse.

In common with others I have had difficulties with relationships. My self-esteem was very low when I was in my late teens and I also had a phase of being quite promiscuous. I desperately needed to belong and be wanted somewhere and rushed into an early and disastrous marriage as a result, although I also managed to get a degree along the way.

My son was born a year after I graduated, when I was two months away from my twenty-second birthday. I wanted him and loved him from the start, but I did find I was very unsure about what to do. This was more to do with being too young and in an unsupportive environment—no one else in our group of friends had children—than to do with my own childhood, but it made me feel quite insecure about my own parenting ability. My mother was of little help—she lowered my self-esteem further by criticizing me. This was a direct result of coming from a very dysfunctional family, as my mother had been unaware of the abuse and had put my difficult behavior down to my being a difficult child. Full stop. So I didn't have a reliable pattern to look back to—but I *did* know that the last thing I wanted to do was to repeat my own family's patterns so I looked for alternatives—I read and I tried to get in touch with my own instincts. I also met other mothers with young children and I watched them and asked them about what they were doing. I developed my own model for bringing up children, which was very much based on responding to the child, rather than following some regime, and on common sense. If he was hungry I fed him, if he seemed bored with something I let him find something else he wanted to do while ensuring he was safe, clean, warm and healthy! I read to him, talked to him, took him out and tried to make his environment secure, happy and stimulating.

The biggest drawback was that my marriage was disastrous and I was myself unsupported, but had little idea that this was the case as I didn't know what being supported meant. My emotional resources were not always up to my son's needs and sometimes I felt that his demands were limitless and would use my own resources up completely. To some extent I overcame this by allowing other people—my mother, my sisters and friends—to be close to him. I felt that I was inadequate and that he should be able to have access to as many loving adults as possible. This was quite successful—he became very confident in his relationships (and has remained that way). Another major problem was that his father was very immature and totally uninterested in him—it was like being a one-parent family with another person also making demands on me which ignored my son's needs. Initially I stayed because I thought I shouldn't split the family. Eventually I realized that it was essential for my own emotional well-being and my son's that I left, which I did when he was six. I believe that my too early marriage to someone uncaring and immature was a direct result of my own need for security and belonging, coupled with very low self-esteem. I came to understand this through the painful experience of a failed marriage and the knowledge that my son was suffering, and I learned from it.

I believe this was a legacy from my childhood: my choice of partner was based largely on the belief that no one else would have me and that he was an artist! My own son has totally different expectations of his relationships—for a start he is not desperately clutching at any sign of warmth and security, because he has those in his family. However, I did learn. My second marriage has been characterized by good communication and caring supportiveness, which my son has also benefited from. This was not luck, but a result of my own growing understanding that I had been abused both as a child and as an adult and my determination never to allow it to happen again. I demanded more and got more—and worked for it.

It has taken time and a lot of painful effort to work through and heal the wounds, and because I was so young when my son was born, he has suffered for my mistakes. I did not understand normal childhood and wanted him to grow up too quickly, then I became overprotective because he didn't! I thought you had to become adult as soon as possible in order to protect yourself, because that is what I had done. Therapy helped me to understand it and to change. My son has needed longer to grow up than he should have done because he had to spend time battling with me for his independence and his right to be a child—but he won and I learned!

I do not think my son came through unscarred, but they are largely scars and not unhealed wounds and they were not suffered as a result of an uncaring parent using him for their own ends, but as a result of a caring parent's own inadequacies and mistakes—and surely all of us are vulnerable to those. Sadly I was not able to have more children—another, indirect, legacy from my childhood (scarring and blockages of the fallopian tubes due to pelvic inflammatory disease during my first marriage), but I believe that had I been able to in the supportive environment of my second marriage I should have made a very adequate parent. As it is, I am able to enjoy the company of friends' children and to experience something of what childhood should and can be. I am not bitter—most of the time—although sometimes I am aware of what I have lost, but then I do not know anyone who has not experienced pain and loss during their lives, so I do not feel exceptional. I do feel, though, that survivors should be able to seek help openly and to find support to enable them to overcome the problems with bringing up their own children and that they should not be stigmatized as being unfit parents, as this is so patently untrue.

CAROLINE

## The family

In seclusion,
one world the family.
Private language, hidden rules, unhealthy ripples—
Something going on.
Childhood's golden, laughing bubble burst.
Blown through the sunlit grass—lost.
Suffocated, grasped, defiled.
Its rules, its power still policing this ghostly outcast from afar.
Consuming all protest.
Sucking my guts dry.

JULIE COCKBURN

## Challenges

For me my marriage and having children were the challenges. I so badly wanted a happy family unit which I'd only dreamed of, but never experienced at first hand. What I did throughout my life was collect what I saw from other families: all the good things. Whether or not they were that didn't matter, I knew no better. I was determined that my own family would be nothing like the one I had grown up in. I learned a lot of skills of my own, and could quite easily put these into practice. I was quite self-sufficient. I felt quite often the resentment from my husband towards me in that area. And I would cruelly use that against him, telling him I didn't love him, didn't need him, in fact hated him. I didn't need anyone or anything. I was so cold and so hard. I would lose control so often, and shout at him, and also my first child—they both got the brunt of the anger I had pent up inside me towards my mother whom I hated. An abuser who I felt nothing for. Cos I suppose if I'd felt I would relive the past and it hurt too much. I could cry for anyone else but me. The practical side of family life came so easy to me: we had no debts, plenty of food, very nice, very clean home, our own. I'd always worked. I was never able to do anything for me. I rarely treated myself, I didn't deserve it.

PAULA LEACH

JANINE GUICE

## Open letter to a mother

Dear Mum,

I have accused you of failure. Failure to protect me, failure to support me, failure to understand me, failure to love me as I think you should. I believe as your child I have the right to accuse you. But, as your daughter, in all these things I have failed you.

By going back to the beginning I understand.

All women are the daughters of women.

I despised you for marrying a man who had been mentally and physically abused by his father and punished us all for his suffering. You were eighteen. How could you have realized the implications? I hated you for being so passive—your acceptance of the constant undermining and the regular humiliations.

I didn't understand your fear of the power and the strength of men. I didn't understand your reasoning that you were fortunate to have a husband generous with money and who didn't beat you. I hated you for not leaving him, particularly after we had all left home and there was no reason that I could see for you to stay. I didn't understand the social climate of those days which made outcasts of divorced and separated women. I can remember the stigma attached to unmarried mothers, but have become accustomed to the choices regarding pregnancy that women now have. I didn't realize that you were afraid to live alone. You'd never had the opportunity to be responsible just for yourself. For most of your life you have been someone's sister, someone's wife or someone's mother.

I hated you for not putting me first. Whoever put you first? Who put your needs before anyone else's? Your education was denied you because you were the eldest and a girl. When Grandfather was killed during the war it was you that had to leave school and look after your brothers and sisters so that Grandma could go to work to keep the family together. No one would have dreamt of halting Uncle John's education if he'd been the eldest. You had been clever and talented at school, particularly in English and music. Have you ever recovered from the disappointment of not being allowed to continue your studies?

You were rewarded for the mothering of your youngest brother by his abuse of your daughter. I am trying to understand your silence about that abuse. Nothing could change what had happened—if no one spoke of it you could pretend it never had—except that the unspoken knowledge has created a barrier between us. Sometimes we have pretended that the barrier does not exist, but as soon as I think for a fleeting moment that I could rely on you to support me during an important phase in my life that barrier leaps up and I search frantically for a weapon to wound you as deeply as I can. It is difficult to realize that all the hurts we have flung at each other over the years originate from that single act of betrayal. The nightmares have stopped now. Those terrifying re-enactments of trying to escape by running through mud which gets thicker and thicker until it overwhelms me with the screams buried in my throat unable to surface. They have been replaced with a recurring dream where I tell you that Uncle Daniel has abused me. It is the day after the first time and I am eleven years old. I am snuggled up to you and I am crying. You have your arms around me with one hand gently stroking my hair. Tears are streaming down your face as you tell me how upset you are that it has happened. You tell me how lovely I am, how good I am, how pleased you are that I have told you. You thank me for trusting you to sort it out. You promise that it will never happen again and you will speak to Uncle Daniel and tell him how angry you are with him and how wrong and unforgivable his actions were. He will no longer be regarded as a member of our family and he must never come to the house again. I will never, ever have to see him.

If only it had been like that.

I have tried so hard to know why I couldn't tell you after the first incident. Why did it have to go on for four years before I could tell anyone? Even then it wasn't you I told but Aunt Lydia. She sensed how uncomfortable I was when Uncle Daniel was around and coaxed the dreadful truth from me. Everything seemed as if it would be all right again. Sitting in her cozy kitchen drinking cocoa I really believed that the dragon would be slain.

Aunt Lydia took me home and told me to stay in the kitchen while she went to talk to you and Daddy in the sitting room. As soon as she opened the door I heard Uncle Daniel's voice and something exploded in my head. I pushed past Aunt Lydia hysterically, to tell you myself. I was spitting with rage as I tried desperately and unsuccessfully to articulate my accusations. Everyone in the room looked dazed and confused. Everyone, that is, except Uncle Daniel. He had this hurt, disappointed expression on his face. Shaking his head sadly, he said I was a nasty, disgusting little girl and how could anyone believe that he could possibly do such a thing. He promised my parents and Aunt Lydia that my allegations were completely untrue and that I must be sick in the head and needed help. Daddy sent me to bed and it is just so incredible that none of us have spoken about it since.

It is only since I gave birth to my own daughter five years ago that I have begun to make sense of the past thirty years, and to have some understanding. This baby was so special and I had looked forward so much to her having a loving relationship with you as I had with your mother. Instead, I couldn't bear you to be around her and I fussed and criticized everything you did for her. The baby appeared very fragile and vulnerable to me and I was totally obsessed with her health and safety to the point of feeling overwhelmed with the responsibility of motherhood. I knew I needed help then but no one listened to me. I wasn't able to say what was really wrong because I didn't know myself. My determination to be the perfect mother with the pristine house and the clean, breastfed baby convinced everyone that I was coping beautifully, but inside I was screaming for someone to recognize my inadequacy and quiet terror.

Now looking back, it is easy to see why I suffered the postnatal depression. Not only did I not trust you or anyone else with my baby because I had felt neglected and betrayed myself as a child, but I didn't trust myself. I didn't trust myself to wake up if she needed me so I didn't sleep properly. I didn't trust myself to have good judgment about people so we have never had babysitters. When Jessica started play group I was in agony at the thought that the helpers would not respond sensitively to her. It is only since she was four that I have relaxed and really enjoyed being a mother. She demonstrates all the time that she knows I love her and that I will always support her. But it is no accident that she is an only child. With all the practicalities involved in parenting I still could not trust myself to provide the same assurance for two or more children. Many people do, I know, but I don't have the confidence. I don't know that I would be better than you were and I have enormous advantages that you have never enjoyed. My marriage is based on equality, my husband shares the housework and childcare and we all treat each other with respect and consideration. If I had not been a victim of child sexual abuse I perhaps would not be so aware of the possibility. Why should you have been aware? It was a taboo subject then. Who knows how I would have reacted in your position, in these circumstances, at that time. There was no evidence—the police would not have taken action.

I know you had strong feelings for Daniel—it must have been difficult for you—which family member to favor? I just wish so much you had chosen me. If only I could have told you after the first time. I know why I didn't. My face is burning and I feel sick just thinking of the horrible things he did to me. I couldn't give you the details now and I am forty, how could I have told you when I was eleven? The bits I told Aunt Lydia were just the tip of the iceberg. Ironic, though, that if I had said the same things when I was eleven I know you would have believed me. By the time I was fifteen you must have wondered what the hell I would do next. You had three other younger children to take care of as well as this sullen, moody girl who was always playing truant, smoking, swearing and running away. Her behavior was the only language she had for the unspeakable and I can't blame you for not understanding it.

I don't mind you having the missing piece of me now. If you didn't have it your life would have been intolerable. I will touch the ragged edges of the space it leaves within me to remember and be grateful for your struggles. You gave as much as you were able, the surrender of more would have meant your destruction. My sufferings were not caused by being your daughter. They were caused by being my uncle's niece and I lay my burden of pain, shame and guilt entirely at his feet. I refuse to carry it any longer or punish anyone else with it. I love you.

Your daughter,

Alice

ROS BARBER

## It's not that . . .

It's not that I don't trust you enough to tell you.
I don't know how.

It's not that I enjoy feeling pain
It's been so long. I don't know anything else.

It's not that I don't want your care, your support.
I've been alone for too long
Yet I'm screaming for it.

It's not that I intentionally shut myself off from you
I'm trapped within my own isolation and fear.

It's not that I don't love you
I love you so much it cuts me in two.

ANNA

---

When you have been sexually abused as a child and you hold the
secret within you, look at other children playing and laughing,
wishing you were truly the same as them, instead of taking on the
role of an actress in a play, pretending you are happy when you feel
so sad inside.

MARGARET KINGDOM

## Martin

I AM CAROLYN
I AM A YOUNG DISABLED WOMAN
I HAVE BEEN HURT A LOT IN MY LIFE
I NEVER THOUGHT I WOULD ENJOY THE COMPANY
    OF A MAN
I MET A MAN CALLED MARTIN
I MET HIM WHEN I UNDERWENT THERAPY FOR
    SEXUAL ABUSE
I FELT SAFE WITH HIM
I WAS CARED ABOUT
I WAS MADE TO FEEL SPECIAL
I WOULD HAVE LIKED HIM TO BE MY DAD
I LOVED HIM
I ENJOYED TOUCHING HIS FACE
I ENJOYED BEING HELD
I DIDN'T AGREE WITH EVERYTHING HE DID
I WAS ABLE TO DISCOVER MYSELF WITH HIM
I DISCOVERED THE TRUE MEANING OF FEELINGS
I LIGHT A CANDLE AND I FEEL CLOSE TO HIM
I SEE A LOG FIRE AND MY MEMORY RECALLS BEING
    TOUCHED NON-SEXUALLY BY HIM
I LOST A BABY
MARTIN WAS VERY GENTLE WITH ME
I HAD MY TEARS WIPED AWAY
I HAD MY FACE STROKED
I AM FEELING SAD
I WANT HIM TO COME AND HOLD ME
I HAVE A SPECIAL BOX AND A BOOK CALLED *RUBY*
    TO REMIND ME OF THE SPECIAL TIMES
I MISS HIM
I LOVE HIM LOADS
I FEEL AS THOUGH PART OF ME IS MISSING
I AM CAROLYN

CAROLYN LOUISE UPTON

## Testing my friend's feelings

I know I test the bounds of our friendship, but it's how I've learned to survive. I know I care for my friends, but do they feel the same way too? Because no one tells me they care for me, I feel so insecure. No one's ever told me they loved me.

It's hard for me to express my inner feelings with someone I feel close to. But I feel so safe when I'm around my friends. I know I care for them but as I've not been used to expressing how I feel, I do not know how to cope, or show how I feel, without feeling scared and ready to run away.

I do not mean it intentionally, to always test their feelings for me, but I still feel a little unsure about what they think of me. I have asked them to try and tell me as truthfully as they can, how they feel.

I tend to find love in everyone, as that's what I need to feel around me. But then I start to cling to these feelings and it doesn't help resolve my long-term insecurity. No one in my family ever showed me they loved me, except when they abused me. I have to rid myself of this type of abusive love and learn to love without pain, anger and fear.

JOAN MARY SIMPSON

## Alone; as part of a crowd

"No one likes me round here."
The thought keeps going round in my head.
I used to sit alone, just
Working or reading a book
My curtain shut; a barrier to show
I didn't belong.
I didn't fit in, they didn't want me.
There was no one to laugh with or cry with
No one to listen, no one to care.

It used to hurt me
Formed a lump in my throat.
I wanted to belong so badly.
I hated myself;
Was it something I'd done?
Something I'd said?

Now, things are different. I can
Sit with them, go round with them
Work with them, talk to them
Share laughter and sadness
With someone who cares.

They're always there to back me up
And to help when I'm in need
Now that I belong.

KERRILEE BARRETT


## The survivors only know

### 1

Sat in the corner
Legs drawn up tight
Shudders running through her
Alone in the night
Her mind it won't focus
Confusion, it is rife
How could someone do this
Just shatter another's life
The emotions screaming through her
Causing turmoil in her soul
Leaving shadows in her eyes
On these nights as black as coal

## 2

Guilt for letting it happen
For another's violent act
Although she's not at fault
She can't accept the fact
Shame in the face of the world
In the mirror on the wall
Feeling sick and dirty
And tasting her own gall
Total violation
Of mind and body and soul
She's lost a part of her person
And feels she'll never be whole
Hate for the bastard
The maker of this hell
Who tore her world apart
And he knew it well
Fear of loving another
For in his eyes she'll see
Reflected memories of pain
That should never be

## 3

The paradox is complete
She considers suicide
Maybe it would have been easier
If she had just died

## 4

But in among this chaos
Friends she has found
Fighting a turmoil all their own
For peace they are bound
They ask of her only

What they give in return
Companionship and care
Happiness to relearn
Each step has its pressure
And to help her there are friends
As an anchor to each other
They will make it in the end

5

With help she has survived
And lives from day to day
Rebuilding from the start
The life of yesterday

MANDY

## Rowena

When my mother took me to visit her mother
Rowena and I were like driven horses
passing in the street.
"Hi," she said, "I got these."
The roomette was crammed with murder magazines.
"See, see. See what he did." Fascinated, furious,
jabbed with her finger at the pictures
(humdrum with age and cheap printing)
of women's bloated bodies half on sofas,
a permed earringed head cut from ear to ear,
the wound black as paint,
women with their legs askew,
their privates, bellies, breasts cut open,
spilling sagging grapey meat on to
dark collared dresses polkadotted white;

grown-up women, very plain,
what's done to them is for all the world to see.
We were just kids. My mother called me to go home.
I patted her shoulder she sat on her bed
hair lanking down "Bye" poring over them.
"She's not right," the mother apologized.
All the way home my mother went on about
those sort of people stinking of cabbage;
but Rowena and I were like driven horses
sharing a burden in a passing glance.

JULIA BRIDGE

## Sexuality

Darkness,
Deep and unknowing
Hidden within me.
Colors merging,
Tangled,
Ripped.
The red of blood
Pouring from me.
The deep blackness
Of tearing flesh.
Nothing is clean and pure,
Nothing is free.
The evil slowly rots—
Layer upon layer
Of death and fear,
Numbing my body.
All sensation is gone
Except pain.

And I know,
This place is not mine,
But was stolen long ago,
And locked away
Buried.

PENNY K.

## Men

Men are the drug of my life, my only salvation. It is they who took away my innocence and distorted, damaged my sexuality. Therefore it is they, and only they who can restore me to normality, a statistic in a well-publicized piece of media mockery that dictates the way women are. How am I? Strange dictation when I don't even know. And, if I do know they never ask anyway, and if they do ask I know they can't really want to know.

How can I let innocence be drawn into the dungeons of loneliness and know where hope has been reduced to a circling spider in his spiral web and love is the smell of rotting flesh? To let them in, to let them even peek into the darkness beyond would be violating their innocence. Their ignorance. And that is wrong. It happened to me and it is wrong.

Besides, how can you explain what a smell looks like? Or what a color feels like? That is how difficult it is to explain the beating of my heart—that ticks with the blissful boring monotony of a clock waiting for the battery to end.

Men.

They came into my life in a steady flow. One by one. Sometimes two by two. All different shapes and sizes and colors and ages. Yet they are all the same because they are men. They reach out for me, intrigued and then back away, confused. I know. Oh yes, I know what they think for I think it too.

In the more serious moments when my sheets only smell of me and darkness is my only companion I lie and try to touch my inner core. But I cannot, for there is a waterfall of tears that threatens to break the backbone of my little life.

I know not how to see myself, nor how men see me. All I know is that they want me, and so do I. I want me. Well, some of them want me and some of me wants me. But the rest stands back, sensibly, for it seems to know my secret, but it's not telling.

TIGRIDIA SYME

## Sexual fears

A fear of not getting it right, not getting it up, coming too soon, not coming, her not coming, me coming before she comes, wanting to wash immediately after coming; of actually liking the neatness of condoms, of drowning in her come, of having to keep doing it until I get it right, of being clumsy, of getting the wrong rhythm, not finding the clitoris, of hurting her, of being too hard or too soft or not being there; of wanting and not wanting anal sex; of being disgusted and fascinated by my want; of getting and regretting my want; licking and having my bum-hole licked, fearing hepatitis B; of being confused; of being fascinated by descriptions of sex and violence; of being horrified by my fascination; of reading and avoiding reading about the fascination and watching it and avoiding watching it and the adolescent fumblings and wanting to do everything but penetration and losing my virginity in a Singapore brothel where I watched from the ceiling knowing I would be punished and the pain at the special clinic when the nurse stuck a swab down my penis and I was pronounced clean but not really believing it and years later thrush stuck and stayed, irritating its way as an ever-present jagging reminder of all my sexual sins, immune to Sporanox, Nystafoam, Canestan and some quack Australian pills from a King's Cross pharmacist with a stereotypic sexist chatline which cost a fortune. It travelled with me from London to the Midwest of America on to Hawaii through Asia and all the way back to London and in the end I surrendered and embraced celibacy and the single bed and gained my comfort from the cellular phone which I cradled to my ear and an occasional bout of hand-jobbing neatly into a carefully arranged pile of tissues to be flushed immediately down the loo so I could pretend it had never happened and I could reminisce about all my past partners from the time at school when such things mattered though we haven't grown much since then in any department recalling the occasional burst of mutual masturbation and nothing ever developed later because when men fancied me, my fear of them, liberally laced with Australian homophobia, meant I fled and years later when I was prepared to consider offers, there weren't any.

RON WIENER

## Challenges: I bought my sexual freedom with my everyday life

Imagine it's night. You're walking down a poorly lit unfamiliar street. You're alone. You hear rustlings behind you. Footsteps? *No,* just rustlings. Your heart beats faster, the skin on the back of your neck prickles . . .

Now imagine feeling like that every night. Heart pounding, neck prickling. But you're not out on the street. You're at home, in your own bed. There is no moment when you're home safe, slamming the door and bolting it behind you. Home. Safe. Hah. For a survivor, the one place that should have been a retreat never has been. The big challenge I face as an adult is learning to feel safe. Every night.

Incest interferes with my everyday life. I don't walk around in a state of universal fear—my life is too short, too valuable. Instead I feel a constant, nagging irritation that what that man did to me for sixteen years still places obstacles in my path. Feeling safe, feeling I'm worth something, feeling I deserve a happy, fulfilled, *sexual* life, overcoming agoraphobia—they don't just happen, they have to be learned. The challenge is learning, even when you don't think you can.

I don't live in constant fear of being assaulted—memory doesn't work that way. Fears become blurred, assimilated, incorporated into everyday life. I lived under my abuser's roof for eighteen years, knowing that *something was wrong,* but I did not, could not, know what. I dreaded the trappings—lying in bed, the smell of tobacco, men in suits, the sound of the radio, the sight of people drunk, vomiting. In my life, I can't avoid these things. Mostly I've just braved it out, paid the price in my everyday life.

The price? I've been agoraphobic for five years—but let's drop the idea right now that I could have, or would want, someone to take over the running of my life for me until I'm "better." I need to eat, sleep, buy food, work, so I handle my fears about going out. How? Meticulous planning, mainly. Half an hour psyching-up time to leave the flat, half an hour to coax myself into bed. I pack bags, make lists, write reminders. When I have to. Otherwise I sweat it out trying to "motivate myself." Recovering for me has been about breaking old habits (of feeling ashamed, fearful, worthless, and so on . . .). But while I'm breaking them, my day-to-day life goes on, I have to deal with suits, drunks, sights and sounds. The challenge is not so much to "cope" as to persuade yourself that just by being here you *are* coping.

One part of my life has remained, surprisingly, intact. Sex, usually a survivor's Waterloo, is for me the one part of my life I'm happy with. Am I alone? Check your healing books: "For a long time I felt like a sexual failure, damaged beyond repair," says one woman in *The Courage to Heal.* "If positive sexuality is my right . . . I don't think I want the right!" says another quoted in *Incest and Sexuality.* This ain't me. I was thirteen when I realized the glint in my father's eye, the rasping of his breath, was sexual (for him). For me, it was abuse. Full stop. My sexual awakening may have been in the midst of a metaphorical house fire, but deep down I knew it wasn't *my* fire. ok, it isn't that simple. Consciously I felt like "damaged goods," dressed in baggy clothes, behaved in any way I could to make it stop. I paid, paid in my everyday life. But some part of me locked my sexuality away intact. I'd been abused since the age of two—the sexual dimension, when I became aware of that, didn't alter the fact that it was abuse.

It didn't just happen that way. As a teenager, I kept my sexual feelings so much under wraps—yes, because I was ashamed of them, but also to say "I won't collude." I was also lucky. I came of age at the height of the mid-eighties AIDS furor: suddenly sexual negotiation was up front, essential, lifesaving. Seeing everyone around me struggling to give fears and feelings voice was like watching them learn a language I had been speaking for years. We have to get good at saying what we want, because for most survivors, keeping shtoom and playing along can give you a flashback. We were of our time. Women of the fifties were supposed always to say no. Those of the sixties and seventies, unerringly yes. In the eighties we began to say "on my terms." For a survivor this was a godsend.

But we survivors are supposed to be dysfunctional, right? We have two choices—either we're easy lays or we avoid sex altogether. We don't have any role models who are survivors and sexually assertive. It's not just me who has noticed. Katie Roiphe, an American also dissatisfied with the sex-danger equation, describes the "easy lay" survivor in *The Morning After*. "The next girl to speak out wears a leather jacket and black jeans. People think of me as a bitch, she says, her voice loud, confident, angry, they think of me as a slut. They think I treat men badly. But she explains that underneath her bitchiness is a gang rape that happened when she was sixteen." Or if we're frightened, frigid, little things, we should either be celibate or lesbians. The ultimate Good Girls.

Well, I'm none of these things. Yes, I've done my fair share of avoiding sex, but aids awareness has been a godsend for me. Safer sex isn't about just latex, but about saying "I'd like X and Y but not Z." It's been about being open about being a survivor with everyone I've been to bed with, whether we've had sex or not. It's been about being able to share fears with male survivors. I've safeguarded my sexuality. Yes, I admit that for me, reckless sex, too-many-beers sex, say-yes-cos-I-dunno-how-to-say-no sex, has never been an option. But check back—getting drunk, being around drunk people is an everyday fear, not a sexual one. But my sexual history has been rather less checkered than those of my non-survivor contemporaries.

In the nineties, a new kind of sexual freedom has emerged: all looks, no action. Flirt outrageously, yet go home alone at the end of the night. Flirting's on, kissing's on, copping's off (so *déclassé*, dear). I found a new kind of sexual confidence. My dress says yes, honey. My behavior says no way. I no longer have to dress and behave to say "leave me alone."

As a survivor, I've had to be sexually assertive. I'd sooner have no sex than why-not sex, don't-care sex, it'll-do sex. So sex has been the one thing in my life that hasn't been a problem. Which is not to say all my partners have been so enlightened. Two, one a survivor himself, asked me why I wasn't a lesbian.

"I've heard forever and ever "Oh, you're a dyke because your daddy did this to you","" seethes one woman in *The Courage to Heal*. "If I'm a lesbian because I was abused, at least something good came of it," responds another. To insinuate a woman is a lesbian because she is a survivor is right out. To insinuate a survivor should be a lesbian is . . . commonplace. Being out on the gay scene (originally as straight, now as bisexual) has been one of the best things that has happened to me—my relationships with women finally improved, and it was women I had learned to distrust. There is no such thing as a "safe" sexual orientation. I was also abused by a woman, so what does that leave me? Celibacy? Is that a "safe" orientation? There is none. Even relationships with other survivors can be racked with misunderstanding. Grow up, sisters, there is no safe place.

Yes, I'm attracted to women and men, and I've had long periods of celibacy while I've been working through these challenges. But the man I have committed myself to is not a survivor. And while once I would on principle sleep only with survivors, now I know that they do not have a monopoly on love, acceptance and patience. I've earned the right to choose my own partner.

In spite of all these challenges, somehow I keep on going. There is no one point when the outside world accepts you, there is no point when these everyday fears become insignificant. But I've paid. And as long as I keep walking down those dark streets, as long as I can still go to bed at night, my everyday life is good enough.

CATRIONA SMITH

---

As we got older my cousin Clare demanded more of me and I felt trapped and unable to tell. I also felt guilty. As a teenager this stopped but I became totally confused about my sexuality. On reflection I now understand why I wanted sex with boys, to see what it was like and whether I was a lesbian, and went "all out" to pretend I liked sex with boys. This preference lasted ten years. I had discarded my virginity by the age of fourteen and by the time I was sixteen I was desperate for love and affection. Other issues were also around at home. My parents had divorced when I was seven and my mother was now at loggerheads with husband number three. Ironically, or maybe not, my next boyfriend I literally lured away from Clare. I eventually married him and this ended in divorce. I stunned the family by not inviting Clare to the wedding but at this time I had actually forgotten why. The details of this did not come back to me until about two or three years ago. I thought I'd just been "playing about." When I was a teenager in the sixties it was easier to say "anything goes," "I believe in free love" than to say no to anyone.

I still feel a little confused about my sexual identity and have not resolved all my feelings about that. What I have gradually searched for and found is respect for myself, not just my mind but my body too. Over the years, including after my divorce, I let men abuse me, not consciously but by not taking control of my life. Later, I really believe I came into the helping professions to resolve inner conflicts. What I have learned now is that I no longer have to feel a fraud, someone pretending to be a good person, a helper, "middle class." I can be and am myself, "warts and all."

ANONYMOUS

JANICE GUICE

## The survivor's song

Because when the world's falling about me
I remember your birthday or your parents' wedding
    anniversary.

Because when I'm crying inside
I shout and scream aggressively and pick a fight with you.

Because I can't hold on to an angry thought
or a hope or a dream, for more than a minute.

Because I trust you about as much as I trust
my cat with a bird, and that is to say about as much
as I trust anyone who isn't me.

Because of all these reasons you,
my partner, should know me and my past,
even though I may not be able to explain
nor know it fully myself.

And you should understand that I can't tell you
how to make it better or
how to teach me to trust you or
how to get near me when I push you away.

I can only tell you
what little I know
and that is all that you see
and that is, how I survived.

GILL CARTER

# Dad

He looked at her
As no dad does
He backed away in shame.

From her shapely hips
She longed for his love
But turned away
from his gaze.

Something was wrong
But, what, she couldn't say!

RUK ESAT

# Just talking

Just talking, making conversation.
Avoiding raw nerves.
No sex talk—YUK!
Boring boring
Depressing whoever I'm talking to
NOT FITTING IN
Feeling uncomfortable.
Smiling in the wrong place
People finding me unbearable
These are my difficulties
Living with people my own age
In this children's home

"CARLA"

## Why me?

When I get up somebody wants
Me to do this or do that.

When I go to work somebody wants
Me to do this or that.

When I was small it was
*Him* who wanted me to do this or that.

All my life I have had to do
This or that for someone.

I wish for once in my life
I could just do what I want
Just for me.

PATRICIA

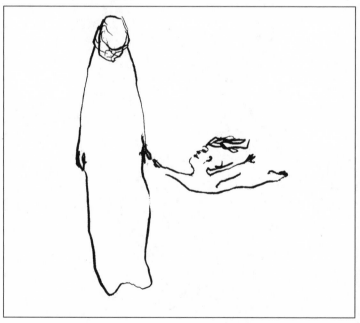

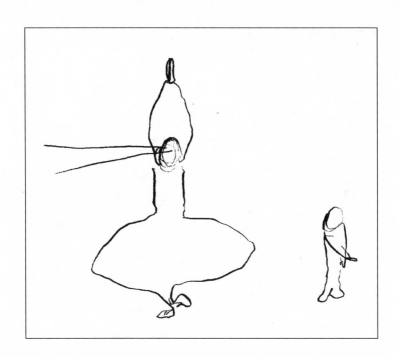

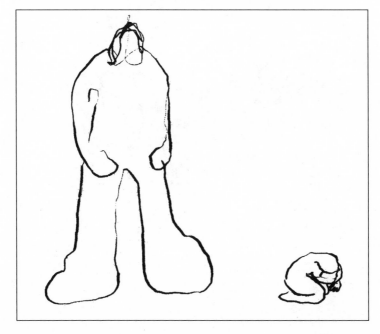

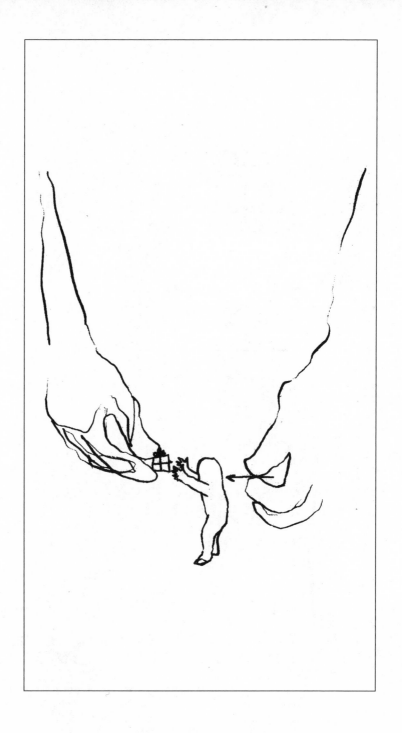

# Claiming the right to feel pain

"Claiming the right to feel pain" is a chapter about survival. In contrast to "The blades of my Life," which describes the feelings and experiences of pain, here the contributors reflect upon some of the strategies that many of us have adopted in order to survive. When the pain and the re-membering of sexual abuse are brought together, it often brings about a set of responses that are unacceptable to many. The survival strategies described here may be seen by many of those who do not understand us as being unacceptable, and as further evidence of our damaged-citizen status. What is little understood is that cutting-up, bulimia, alcohol, are our reactions to extreme situations and mental anguish. These survival strategies, far from being the damaging actions of damaged citizens, can be a way of controlling or realizing the intangible pain we feel.

Emily Bird, writing on the subject of "Alcohol," states: "Your poison and beguiling kisses comfort me like no other." "Uncomfort-ably numb" describes the ways in which cutting-up is "the wish to al-leviate pain in a familiar yet deadly way."

Penny, in a different voice, takes us through the many strate-gies she employed while growing up, including escaping into the world of fantasy, "seeking out doses of affection and normality" from her friend's family and from teachers, joining in the activities of the local church, through distancing herself and through work.

So, while a number of the pieces that are included here describe thoughts, feelings and actions that many may have difficulty in un-derstanding in other than negative terms, for us these are all part of a wider and more positive agenda: survival.

My stepsister had just started training to be a nurse in a town about forty miles away and this is what planted the seed in my head.

To do my nurse training would mean having a job that was far enough away to necessitate me leaving home. So I applied to do my nurse training, not from any sense of "calling" but simply to get away from home.

This was the best decision I ever made, I found that I loved nursing, it gave me a complete sense of satisfaction. I was doing something that was important and stimulating. I loved everything about it and soon felt that at last I was happy. I could not imagine doing another job now; in fact it is more than a job, I have invested an enormous amount of emotional and physical energy in my profession and it is something that I feel very proud of.

Nursing served several purposes for me; it put me in a situation where I gained self-esteem because I was doing something that was good in everyone's eyes. However, what this also meant was that my sense of self became dependent on whether I was a good enough nurse, and this meant doing that little bit extra, feeling that I had to be more caring than anyone else and needing to be the top of the class to feel good about myself. I realize now that this was not a healthy situation for me to have created, but at the same time I know that I cared deeply about the patients I worked with and that I put every ounce of energy I had into my work.

PENNY

## Alcohol

My friend
My warming glass
My kissing cup
My wassail
Give me heart
When the night is dark

And love is cold
Your poison and beguiling kisses
Comfort me like no other.

EMILY BIRD

*Emily Bird changed her name to dissociate herself from her father, who was a known pedophile.*

## Uncomfortably numb

to dig the blade deep
into the arm and
twist hard

and yet feel nothing
as the spirit is purged

a symbolic expression
of an ancient hurt

in a place where
words are not
possible

the wish to alleviate
pain in a familiar
yet deadly way

primeval suffering is
temporarily anesthetized

as the hunger for
destruction becomes
unbearable

and it is no longer possible
to disobey its commands

ALEX BENJAMIN

## Childhood

Roti and dal
Slither down
My dry throat
Pani to wash it down with
Acrylic and nylon
Cover my skin
Images flicker
On the TV screen
I sit comatosed
Occasionally transferring
To other available islands
Sometimes I dive into books
And sit hidden
Amongst the characters' wordplay
Silent amongst their drama
I nestle craftily behind a settee
Or within the folds of the curtains
Sometimes I perch on top of the lampshade
And watch Little Women, Famous Five or
The Wombles.
Later come Cathy and Jane Eyre.
As I grow older
These childhood escapes
Branch out into more
Elaborate tales and characters.
But I am still there
On the periphery,
Faceless and voiceless.

RAMANI

## My box

Here I sit in a box,
It has large thick black walls,
It is very warm and safe,
It has no door or windows,
It has a crack in the wall,
Where I can watch the world.
I have lots of things in my box,
I have some trousers,
In a box within my box,
I have lots of pretty dresses,
To keep me company
I have creativity
Which no one understands.
The walls of my box inside,
Are painted with blood.

When no one is looking, I can leave my box,
        no one can ever enter my box.
I sometimes come out of my box,
        for special people
Sometimes men, sometimes women,
I attach a piece of string to my box
        when I leave it,
Each piece of string has three knots,
        one for each betrayal,
On the third betrayal of each person,
        I re-enter my box,
I will never come out again for that person.

It's a safe box, but it's lonely.

SHARON SPARHAM

## Invasion of body/soul/mind/space

Manchester
Chorlton Library
SANCTUARY
Hiding amongst the bookshelves
Not very safe
But safe enough to say to him
"I've gone to the library."
Escape in study
Studying to escape.
Meantime
Temporary escape.
My eyes glazed
I stare at the blurred titles.
I search haphazardly for blind corners,
Where I can collapse
And cry.
Where I can go and let "it" go
Release "it."

He touches my arm
I jump and take my arm away.
"You look sad," he says
I stare back.
"You look very depressed."
My energy seeps away from me
As he moves closer, entrapping me,
Staring at me.
I do not speak.
The stranger continues . . .
"Can't you speak? . . .
You're well gone . . .
Go and see a doctor, darlin'
Are you suicidal . . .
Need any help?"

I stare at him
I stare at him

Then I punch him in the face

I speak and I say
"Piss off . . . this is my time and
    my space."

RAMANI

---

What kept me going?
A hope, a dream?
Wishful thinking?
Faith, hope, charity, love?
Soup kitchens, books?
Drugs and sex?
The color of eyes?
The arm of the law?
Blind justice?
Bloody-mindedness?
In the Garden of Remembrance
    there are my papa's ashes.

AIRB

## Safety

I do not like
Men:
Large,
Angry,
Loud,
In groups
Or any people in authority.

I need to control—
A room,
A bed,
A car,
An income,
A fuck,
A job.

How else,
Do I make the world safe?

RON WIENER


## Bleeding

As I watch blood ooze from my vein
Slowly the droplets anesthetize my brain.
The screaming in my head gently subsides
Calmed and sedated, almost mesmerized.

I am losing the struggle to survive.
I have to bleed to know I'm alive.
The tramlines of war scar my skin
The only sign of the battles within.

My life drips on to the barren floor
Tears flow in rivulets under the door
Numbness spreads right through my core.
Where is my energy to fight for more?

But these are cuts not for death but life
Do not be alarmed at the way I strive
Marks on my body are a small price to pay
For freedom from Hell and a new dawning each day.

PHILL

## Dissociation

Tick tock, tick tock, SCREAMS the ornamental clock,
Tick tock, tick tock, will this TORTURE ever stop.

Tick tock, tick tock, pounding CEASELESSLY in my brain,
Tick tock, tick tock, my life will NEVER be the same.

Tick tock, tick tock, the pain is going to drive me MAD,
Tick tock, tick tock, the WORST experience I've ever had.

Tick tock, tick tock, IGNORE it, it will go away,
Tick tock, tick tock, you SURVIVE to face another day.

Tick tock, tick tock, all ALONE I plead to know why,
Tick tock, tick tock, when will this all end and I can just DIE.

Tick tock, tick tock, ON and ON and ON and ON,
Tick tock, tick tock, pushed to the floor my SANITY gone.

I managed to survive my sexual abuse by means of dissociation. The assaults practically all took place in the same room which contained an old clock on the mantelpiece. This clock had a very loud and distinctive sound. I used to concentrate on the ticking of the clock to avoid listening to my abuser's bestial satisfied grunting as he raped me. The best definition I ever heard of dissociation was "the suspension of reality." This suspension of reality enabled me to deal with a situation and emotions so overwhelming to me at that early age. Its legacy has, however, haunted me for twenty-odd years.

I still find it nearly impossible to relax in an environment that contains a noisy timepiece. It has only begun to ease slightly since I commenced counselling and the haunting effect that kind of abuse can throw up has become clearer. Dissociation is a useful tool to assist survival, but the time has to come when you stick your head above the ramparts and say HELP.

PAUL

BEKKI

## Survival

Looking back on my experiences I can identify many things that I did which enabled me to survive.

As a small child I would read fairy tales avidly and would lose myself in the stories of Cinderella, Rapunzel, Little Red Riding Hood,

The Red Shoes, The Three Bears, the list is endless. I would spend hours reading. This would serve a couple of purposes, the first of which was that if I was reading I was quiet so I wouldn't be annoying my mother and there was less likelihood of me being shouted at or feeling terrified. The second purpose was that these fairy tales instilled hope in me: I believed them so thoroughly and thought that one day something magical would happen to me and that I would be rescued. I spent many an hour imagining being taken away from my home by somebody wonderful who would treat me kindly and would look after me—I really believed this would happen.

Another method of survival during my childhood was to seek out small safe corners where I would receive little doses of affection and "normality." One of these places was next-door where I would play with my friend Claire. Her family was something completely alien to me yet I knew that this was what it should be like. Her mother and father loved her dearly and constantly showed this. I would try to gain some of that love by playing with Claire when her parents were around. They would allow me into their home and her mum would do things like let us help her bake cakes and lick out the bowl when she had spooned the cake mixture into the tins. This may sound a bit strange but it was wonderful to me.

The village vicar was another source of affection. I spent a great deal of time in the church and at the vicarage, I joined the choir, the hand bell group and the tower bell group. All of this meant that I was out of my home and was treated kindly by others. The vicar used to give me fizzy drinks. I particularly liked dandelion and burdock, of which he seemed to have a plentiful supply! In all of these situations I endeavored to be as good as possible, terrified that I might spoil the little attention I was getting, it was so precious.

As I grew older I sought and received affection from my school-teachers, in particular my French teacher and my music teacher, both of whom spent a lot of time with me and invested a lot of energy in my development. I remember once having a migraine during a French lesson: the pain was so bad that I thought my head was going to explode. I began to cry; I did it quietly but my teacher noticed and took me outside, asked me what was wrong and I told him about the pain. He then hugged me—it was wonderful, I felt really cared for. I had never been hugged like this before, it was so gentle and caring, I didn't want it to stop.

My music teacher was equally caring. He took a special interest in me as I had a flair for the violin. During my school years the music department was being rebuilt and he took a photograph of me standing on the foundations of the new block playing the violin. I felt very special.

I loved secondary school. I was liked by most of the teachers and was always treated with respect and kindness. I guess that this was partly due to my need to be liked and subsequent "good" behavior. I did not think that I could be liked just for being me so I put a great deal of effort into getting good grades, being polite and witty.

Humor became a great tool in my life: I found that by amusing people and making them laugh I felt good. I didn't act the fool, but always had something funny to say and a laugh that could be heard for miles! Humor is also a great defuser of anger and tension and I learned that to use it in this way kept me safe when I thought that a situation was brewing. I still have this capacity, but I don't use it to win people's affections any more.

I also recall separating myself from what was going on so that although I could physically feel what was going on, emotionally I was completely numb. It would be like looking at myself from the other side of the room: I could see what was happening but didn't connect with it in my mind. One thing that makes it difficult to remember all the incidents is that he never spoke during any of his attacks, he was completely silent except for the grunts he made while trying to restrain me. I believe this silent approach was very powerful, it was almost as if nothing had happened: no words were exchanged, so it never happened.

PENNY

## Challenges: Claiming the right to feel pain

As a woman who survived sexual and other abuse for the first eighteen years of my life, I feel sometimes that I am in a race against time: my understanding and healing is the Hare; and the Tortoise is my failing health. I am now fifty-two.

My health has been directly affected by what happened to me: I still bear the pains of physical injury. I have been able to acknowledge damage to my spine, and I get osteopathic treatment for it from time to time. But I have somehow felt ashamed to tell any doctor about my lifelong hip joint pains, and have endured in silence great trouble in walking and climbing stairs in winter: I am just beginning to acknowledge this damage. I have found out that it too was probably caused by physical injury.

I believe that another direct effect of my abuse was hypothyroidism. As a child at home, every day was a crisis and my metabolism adjusted accordingly. When I left home and began life in an environment free from constant anxiety and violence, the lack of stimulation caused a hypothyroid crisis; and I have had a struggle ever since with metabolic imbalance including hypoglycemia. (I now treat it homeopathically.)

From when I was fifteen and a compulsive over-achiever at school, I had repeated blackouts from overwork and forgetting to eat and drink. I couldn't stop driving myself. When I was twenty, due to self-neglect (going with a wet head in winter) I got a middle-ear infection and was advised to have an operation or it would trouble me in later life. I ignored the advice—I "didn't have time." Now, more than thirty years and two operations later, it is an incurable, dangerous and debilitating chronic condition. (One day after the first ear operation I wrote a poem to myself. It was called "Hard road, hard rider, soft machine.")

I also have chronic sarcoidosis, an autoimmune disease that seems to be particularly common among survivors of child sexual abuse. It can be controlled but not cured by steroids. Echoing uncertainty and denial, it assumes mimicking forms and may be overlooked for a long time. In my case it was about eight to ten years before it was discovered through the vigilance and persistence of a GP who believes in his patients, and who believed in my right to be well more than I was able to myself at that time.

The indirect effects of child sexual abuse on my health are also extensive. Being abused made me separate my body from myself in self-defense. This separation has taken several forms. I have amnesia for large chunks of my childhood (even after years of therapy), which are still buried and ticking like nuclear waste. Self-hatred has made it impossible at times for me to listen to myself or believe I am important enough to have health needs. Denial has made me simply cut off physical sensation, dismiss pain as "being silly," and value self-neglect as proof that I was strong. Personality splitting—which I experience as a form of amnesia over which I have partial control—has also caused havoc with health needs, making me forget what I have experienced and said, when to take medicines and so on; and it has contributed to bad relations with doctors. The social isolation I have experienced as a secondary effect of abuse has cut me off from care, support and feedback about my health, among other things.

Studying these indirect effects is discovering an inner process that is a revelation to me. The abuse that happened to me made me develop protective mechanisms which were appropriate at the time and may have saved my life. They were adaptations that denied or deferred my own needs, which hardened over time into outdated neurotic patterns. They included not believing in love of any kind, and faking affection; not believing in my beauty; not believing in my pain.

I was a traveler, to whom movement was safety, search, escape and distraction. I was a tough nut who had babies without crying, opened jam jars for strong men, could cope with anything for any length of time. I treated myself worse than any machine. Being of mixed race, I iconized my black shard of race and culture as the sole source of my strength. But that strength was an illusion, based partly on rejection of my weakness and my need, like a building with all the best work in its façade and a hovel behind. I thought I was indestructible then: a sign, as I know now, that I could not hear my body's voice.

Without information about the extent and nature of my abuse as a child, I always knew that there was something wrong, like an invisible burden that I carried everywhere, and when I was forty-eight I was lucky enough to find the therapy (person-centered) and the therapist that I needed. After four years' hard work and a successful transition, my therapist said "I will always remember you as the child who didn't know that she had the right to feel pain."

Illnesses have dogged my life. From where I am now I can trace the origins of many of them to my abuse as a child, indirectly through damage to the normal mechanisms of self-love, memory and feedback. From my own experience I believe that we need to re-examine the way that child sexual abuse may affect many aspects of our health by damaging the feedback mechanism. If we can learn the lessons from this we may gain control over a crucial area of our lives: health is empowerment, and ill health is continual disempowerment.

I am not "cured." Who's perfect? I am like a stunted tree, scarred but alive, still bringing forth new leaves from time to time. I am at university now, getting my long-delayed education. For the first time I am in control of my life; and I have plans! My health is delicate and probably always will be. It acts as a reminder to take my body seriously. Taking good care of myself, listening to my physical needs, is a way of defying the odds that were stacked against me, and beating them. It is a way of giving thanks that I am alive. It is a way of expressing what I think of my life today: it's exciting, it's unique, it's a life that I would not exchange for any other in the world: the life of a survivor.

JULIA BRIDGE

# Pulling things from a dark cupboard

"Pulling things from a dark cupboard" is about remembering. In her poem, which provided the inspiration for the title of this chapter, Janine expresses remembering as a need to address that which is hidden, even if we know the hidden to be ugly and painful. Janine's "dark cupboard," the place where those painful memories are stored, has also been described as an "assassin in the dark" in "My first year as a known survivor." Lizzie Cottrell, in "Don't," describes the terrifying feeling of knowing that there is something "there" but desperately wanting it to remain where it is.

The contributors to this chapter also demonstrate the multiple and confusing ways in which remembering the abuse works its way out as memories of all kinds: memories that affect emotions, show in our actions, work on our bodies and haunt us at night-time. In putting this chapter together we have tried to reflect our diverse responses to remembering. "The nightmare—that's true" describes the ways in which the author is transported back to the scene of the abuse through her nightmare, in which she experiences a powerful and almost palpable re-enactment of the original assault.

Another important layer of the remembering is tackled in this chapter through an exploration of the highly complex, and thereby often misunderstood, realm of the links between remembering and forgetting. Beth, in "The forgetting (and the remembering)," provides a vital glimpse into the abused child's thought processes. First through the original process of forgetting—which remembering sets out to counteract—and then through the creation of a fantasy world which is safe to inhabit, to replace the vacuum the forgetting generates.

An anonymous contribution, "Surviving abuse: my story," describes the way in which forgetting was used as a mechanism for survival following the largely unhelpful reactions of others that served to compound the negative effects of the initial abuse. We are left with the poignant message that for this author there was nowhere left for her to go—except into the forgetting.

———————

## Don't

Don't

Don't

Rope the hope cover the night
bury the hung
sawdust the blood
stardust the blood
cover the blood.

Don't
remember.
Never never never
don't ever
ever remember.

DON'T

LIZZY COTTRELL

---

Daddy at the pub
Mummy in the club
Baby's tied to the bed
Nothing to be said

Thirteen lying dead
Lost inside my head
Lots of life's blood shed
Nothing to be said

Is this in my head
Daddy's in my bed
Innocence is dead
Nothing to be said

On the theater bed
My heart filled up with dread
Now the baby's dead
Nothing to be said

Hunger never fed
Faces always red
Waiting to get wed
Nothing to be said

Divorce is where it's led
No one ever said
In my heart I'm dead
Nothing to be said

Awakening in my head
All the memories shed
I'm no longer dead
Something to be said

MEA ROSS-SIMMONS


# Like razor blades

Crashing day of thunder
pounding through my head—
touching time of danger
another day to dread.
Touching my weakness
lightening of shame
thoughts flash by with
silver blades
cutting through my veins.

SELINA NICHOLAS

J. K. HORN

## Surviving abuse: my story

I think that both my parents found it hard to show me any affection. I can't remember either of them holding me or showing me any physical affection if I was upset. If I fell off my bike, or fell over, I was expected to be brave. I would be given sweets or money as a reward for being a big girl and not crying. If I did cry, my mother would tell me to stop making such a fuss.

My mother was frequently angry with me as a small child, especially if I was too noisy or messy in my play. She would scream at me and fly into a rage, and say that I would have to be punished to teach me how to behave. She would hit me with a belt. It made me feel even more guilty and ashamed of myself. I felt exposed to the world and thought that all the neighbors would know how bad I was.

I think I was about six or seven when my dad started coming into my room at night. He would start by gently stroking my back and I would feel relaxed and comforted. But then I remember him pulling up my nightdress and I turned my head and looked at my wallpaper, which I could just make out in the half-light. I really hated that wallpaper, but it was better to focus on the wallpaper than to look at him as his face had changed. It would be kind of scrunched up, and he would be looking right at me but didn't look like my dad. His hand would be between my legs and he would rub me. I tried not to feel anything, but I couldn't stop myself. It felt nice, and even though I felt ashamed I didn't want him to stop.

Eventually, my mother must have found out what was happening, although I don't know how. I can remember her coming into my room after he had gone. She would take me into the bathroom and take my nightdress off. I would then have to sit on the edge of the bath with my legs open and she would put a toothbrush inside me to clean my insides. She would tell me that my insides were all mashed up and I'd never have children, and that I was dirty and bad and needed to be punished. Then she would put my nightdress back on and send me back to bed. I would then lie awake praying to God to let me die, and would cry for hours until I eventually must have fallen asleep.

I can remember trying to tell a teacher when I was about eight or nine, but she got angry and shouted at me and told me to stop making up lies. Some of the other children heard her shouting at me and thought I must have been naughty. They then started teasing me about this as I was a real swot at school and was never in any trouble. I can remember leaving the classroom after being shouted at by the teacher feeling terrible and wishing that I was dead.

When I was ten, something inside me seemed to change. I could no longer cope with what was happening, and just knew that I had to do something drastic if I was to survive. It is as though I became a different person as I convinced myself that life was perfect: I had wonderful parents and lots of friends. My body shape seemed to change and I felt far less ugly than before, and I made an effort to be like everyone else and fit in, even though I knew it was an act. But it is as though the act somehow became reality, and I forgot everything about my other life. By the time I went to secondary school, all the awful things which had been happening to me had stopped, and for years I had no memories at all of this past life, as I had made myself forget everything.

ANONYMOUS

## Birdie's poems

**1980 (four years before memories began to surface):**

> I built my own cage
> I thought to house a tiger
> And I told nobody how I
> Stood guard all day and night.
> The bars were made of sugar and spice
> Of sanity, smiles and all things nice.
> And I told nobody of how

The smiles froze numb upon my face
And how I wearied in the vigil
How I wished the beast would wake
And trample down its bars and roar
While I joined in, smiling no more
But screaming.

**1984 (just before first flashbacks occurred—this poem came from a dream):**

She is closer
Many nights I heard her crying
Out in the dark
The wind and rain.
Go away little girl
Go back—I do not want to know you.
I drew the curtains
Stoked the fire
Turned up the stereo.
Perhaps she would die
If no one heard
And no one came—
Lie down in a freezing ditch
Curled in a ball
Her whimpers fading
Little body growing weaker
Till she was snuffed out
Silenced for all time.

But she grows stronger.
Now she circles near
And now she cries
With anger in her voice.
She is looking for me.
Go away little ghost
I do not want to know you.

I bolt the door
And lock the windows
Block my ears
But still I hear her
Cannot drown her rage.
My fire burns low
The storm increases
I can no more defend
My sanctuary
No more pretend to ignorance.

Now she quiets
Now she is at the door.
Wait there little girl
I know you
Wait and very soon
I will unbolt the door
And let you in.

EMILY BIRD

## The forgetting (and the remembering)

As a little girl, aged six or seven, I would have what I thought was the most delicious experience, the forgetting, I call it. It would come upon me in ordinary places when I was sitting on the stairs or playing in my secret hideaway, I would feel it coming on and then I would wait, silently anticipating it until it was here. Suddenly, out of nowhere I would forget the name of my town, of the country and of myself. I did not know who I was, where I was, what connection I had with anyone around me. I became no one, nothing, a non-existent speck. Yet far from being frightened, I felt free and content to consider endlessly the reasons for my existence. Sooner or later, however, this feeling of forgetting would leave me. Often, it was because my dog Paddy who followed me patiently would nuzzle me and I'd stroke his silky red ears. "Oh yes, you're Paddy," I'd say. And slowly, with Paddy as my center I'd work my way outwards remembering that this was a planet called Earth, that this country was the us, the town we lived in Springfield, and that my name was Beth, that I was, to my disappointment, simply a real little girl and not an ethereal spirit who floated through the universe. As I got older, these moments of forgetting became less and less, although often I willed and waited for them to occur, disappointed when they didn't. Sometimes, in my teens, I'd ask others if they had the same experience, sure that this was a common childhood experience and when they said no, I felt jarred and unnerved, but I put these feelings aside.

Today, I am an adult in my mid-twenties. A survivor who has been through several years of therapy. I am very sociable, personable, some say larger than life, a laughing loud American among reserved, quiet British. Well defined some might say. Yet as I think back to the experience of forgetting, of remembering how delighted I was to become a non-person, I feel sad for the child I was, a child who felt so fragmented, out of place and alone that she had to literally escape into a world where she did not exist.

As I got older, fantasy took the place of the forgetting. So I could not forget now who I was, but I could create a fantasy land where I could escape to. A land filled with adventurous TV and book characters like Doctor Who and Trixie Belden. In my late teens and early twenties, romantic fantasies about real people (usually older unavailable women like my lecturers) became another escape route allowing me to spend hours with others and in my fantasy life.

Luckily, I did not lose myself entirely. I did not as a little girl end up in a state of permanent forgetting, of isolation. I did not become completely involved in obsessive fantasies, unable to distinguish reality from fantasy. These were (and sometimes are) temporary states I used to escape when I could not cope—when as a child I could not face the reality of my abuse, when I was unable to be heard by others. I am now choosing to become a person who is integrated, who is whole. I cannot completely reject the sad child I was; I must accept the massive sadness that I could not express then, the feelings of aloneness, of wanting to be elsewhere, but at the same time I must value my strength and ingenuity. I am now a person who knows her name, who she is and the many different parts of her, laughing and sociable as well as depressed and sometimes lonely.

BETH (1)

---

I've always seen your outline pass,
Between the weary branches,
Of my tiring mind.

I've always let you go,
Thinking you were just another falling bough,
Resting on my sanity.

But you will not escape again,
I can trap you with my darkness
With my shadows, with my words.

RAE-SARAH HOUSE

## My need to pull things from a dark cupboard

Rectangle shells of wood
fade drum rolls in hollows
inside ice
behind clam shut
the eyes which tried to sleep
the baby haze

Somewhere was a bright light
stabbed through a keyhole
there was no key

no act of turning
to free the frozen

Blinded back to front
unfocused presence
the shadow there
upon my spine
loomed brittle blunt
behind was sore
with searing gaze

"Act well the mime of rest
sweet child," the shadow said
protest has no place in this
a little ticklelooking
game with someone
we won't mention.

Windows watched
tides wash in
the dirts of fear and shame
floods to false horizons
flattened calm
a made-up mask to hide
the keyhole burning

I have a need to pull things from a dark cupboard

they hurt
those shredded smelling garments
worn secret
soiled underwear
worn silent
the ugly dress.

JANINE GUICE

## Sometimes I get real scared

I blank out and I look at the mirror and I see fear and haziness and wasted-awayness and ugliness and I get scared.

I am heavily aware of my body.

My body feels dry.

My body feels full of dirt.

My scalp is irritable and I scratch it until small pieces of skin give way and there is blood underneath my fingernails and blood staining my fingertips. My hair feels lank and greasy and I stare at the small mirror and my face looks diseased and as if it is decaying and I remember my once-only LSD trip and how my face had looked then as it does now, wasting away, and I can see my father's features. I see his face in my face and I try to make it vanish, make it disappear. I try to pull, scratch it away. Tear "it' apart, waste it away. I try to disappear. I try to vanish. Pull and scratch, waste myself away as I tear myself apart.

And I feel dry and itchy. I feel dirty and ugly. My arms are weak and futile. My fingers are nervously anxious and pull at my skin. I am scared but I don't even think about it, I just feel it.

I am panicky and I cannot bear to meet my own gaze in the mirror as it terrifies and upsets me because with it I remember each and every time I locked myself in some bathroom somewhere and stared into the mirror just as I have done now and I remember how terrified and lonely I feel and have felt. I was isolated then and I am isolated now. And I feel that I could die and nothing would happen. And I feel that I could vanish and there would not be a flicker of movement to acknowledge the passing of my existence.

And I think of all the things I wanted to be and what I am and I feel that somewhere along the line my growth has become stunted and diseased and I am unable to develop, unable to move on and I feel as if my head is reeling with words, pictures and stories that I want to tell but no one will hear me. And sometimes I do try to speak loud so that I can make myself heard but my throat feels achy, achy sore and I unable to continue. And I feel like I want to throw up. Only there is nothing left in my stomach.

Ramani

## The nightmare—that's true

I was in a strange house, which seemed to be full of people. People I knew, but I cannot remember their faces. There were a few central figures in this nightmare, one was an older woman. She was the mother of the house. I was not comfortable with her although she was very nice to me. But deep down I knew that she wanted to harm me in some way.

There was also a young man: he had long black hair and was very attractive. I felt very threatened, everything about the atmosphere was pleasant but with underlying tremors of violence. Another man was there, he was the father of the house; I felt very ill at ease with him although again, he was pleasant.

There were lots of rooms in the house and lots of activity. I tried several times to go into the kitchen but each time I tried someone stopped me. There was also one dark and foreboding front room. The longer I was there, the more frightened I began to feel. I was in the living room with the older woman, I was saying that I wanted to go home but she kept making excuses and trying to make me stay longer. She had a wooden spoon in her hand a lot of the time. I was standing up talking, saying to all sorts of people that I wanted to go home but they all kept making excuses. Louise and other people I knew were there sitting on the couch, but they all ignored my pleas.

I saw the older man out of the corner of my eye—he was watching me. The younger man came into the room, he came up behind me and put his hands on my shoulders. I jumped and he laughed, I felt something go through my thighs, his penis. I struggled desperately to get free, but he put his arms around me so that I could not get loose. I was upset and disgusted, looking round at everyone for help but they just laughed at me. I tried to break free but couldn't— I looked down and he ejaculated all over me! I was crying now, I felt so violated and he just rubbed himself and his sperm all over me. I was shaking and sobbing, everyone was laughing hysterically at me. I broke loose and tried to run out of the house, but people blocked me so I ran into a downstairs bathroom. My feelings and emotions were overpowering, I felt so appalled, violated, and disgusted. LOST.

I was terrified of what else they would do to me, I was shaking so much I did not want to go out of the room and see any of these people. I tried to think of a way to escape, but eventually someone came to get me. I felt so angry at these people. I said to Louise "Why didn't you do something?' and she replied "Don't worry about it, it wasn't that bad!' I could not make her see that they had hurt me. I felt absolutely alone and helpless. I kept trying to leave but everyone stopped me, they were all now being very nice to me, but there was still surrounding violence.

I went into the front room, I wanted to do something but all I saw was a room flooded with water and an electric cable in the pool. The old man came and dragged me into the other room and threw me on the settee.

I somehow managed to escape into the street, Louise running after me. I ran up to a bending road to the right—I was being chased. I saw a front door open and someone letting guests out of their house. I ran to the door but the man smiled and tried to shut it. I pushed past him into his house, I started shouting at them to phone the police, when Louise came in. The man just stood there. After I phoned the police, I relaxed a bit, but stayed by the phone. After a while I gathered the police were not coming. As the realization must have shown on my face, the man said something about knowing the people that had attacked me, intimately, and he moved threateningly towards me.

The next thing I was in court: the woman and the old and younger men had been charged with rape and kidnap. They were all found innocent. I was really shocked and then the judge said that he was part of their group. Everyone ran towards me and I tried to run away. They had knives and other weapons. I was very frightened. I had an ice pick from somewhere and defended myself, stabbing at loads of people. I stabbed someone in the eye—it was very graphic with lots of bodies and blood, killing and screaming—somehow I managed to escape.

*Then I woke up.*

SANDRA VEASEY

# Friday 26th November

Children are so vulnerable—they depend totally on the adults around them. How could anybody abuse that trust? Keely clinging on to me tonight made me realize a lot of things. She depended on me to look after her and protect her. At just a year old she can already tell who should look after her. She is totally innocent and anyone could do anything to her without her feeling threatened. Why should she? Why should any child think that adults do things wrong? Something has just clicked. In a child's eyes and mind, adults don't do wrong—they are blameless. At four years old I had no reason to think that he shouldn't have done what he did. He was my daddy. Daddies are wonderful—they don't hurt their children—they just love them. That's what I must have thought—that's what I'd like to think now. I couldn't do anything. I had no reason to think that I should do anything to stop him. If I've been told that once, I've been told a hundred times. It's just taken a one-year-old baby to make me realize it.

I'm still not totally sure why it didn't all come out in the open at some point or other—I can't understand that yet. Could it be that I blocked things out as they were happening? It scares me that I've got no memory of him being around when I was young, apart from the vague recollections of those times that caused so much pain. How quickly could I have forgotten what happened? Why are all the memories coming back now?

JUDITH SEYMOUR

# Memoir of a Doppelgänger[1]

What's wrong with me? I hardly dare even to admit to it. I'm too weird. Why do I avoid people? Why do I tear at my fingernails? Why am I always afraid?

It is as if a tortured god had looked down and said: "I will make you special with these gifts. I will give you the gift of a mind so that you may know my confusion, the gift of sex so that you will know shame, the gift of being so that you may know fear, the gift of a self to know shit, and the gift of bewilderment so that you may not know me.' And there was I, not knowing what the gods had done. What the gods had done was too terrible for me to bear, so I became someone else.

How was I before I recognized that god? Isolated, feeling like a figment of my own imagination, I was usually anxious or afraid but was unable to recognize it. I felt as if I was pretending to be alive. Relationships were difficult and I generally allowed them to fade after diverting them from contact with my self. I ran away from sex. I felt really safe only when on my own but then I often felt lonely.

If anyone asked me how I was I might have said something like "Oh, I haven't really thought about it much, so I guess I must be ok! How are you?" But I spent much of my time thinking about it. I must have spent years trying to work out why I felt so bad, but it did no good. I kept bouncing off that soft wall of amnesia without knowing I had changed direction.

I was without foundation and my feelings were gripped by a hidden hand. Constrained in an invisible vacuum of fear I made a pretense of living, hardly able to breathe. But who was I? Who am I?

Each of us lives from our own history. Our past is part of our present because it shapes the beings we are. We may not have chosen any of this but the choices we now make will not be free of it. Even if you can't remember you still can't forget. Nowadays I feel like a detective trying to track down the missing parts of my soul, as if they belong to someone else. But I know they once were part of me.

A year ago I felt together. I thought that it did not matter that I could not remember what had happened to me so long as I knew something had and that the person I now am is the person whose behavior and feelings I work with. Today I'm not so sure. It's as if I have been swimming along in clear shallow waters and suddenly I feel afraid. I look down and it's very dark, very deep and very real. There are scary monsters down there.

As I understand more of the way I now am, I am able to remember some of the feelings and perceptions of the little boy I was. Somehow acceptance of myself now enables me to better accept the feelings of the past. The past is again part of the present, in the sense that I recall my memories into the awareness I have now, however that colors them. Indeed, starting to know myself today seems to facilitate recall of how it felt then. Although I have, as yet, few memories of specific incidents, mainly just smudges and half-images. I know when they feel real. They feel real today although I carry them from thirty years ago. They are still my experience: thirty hours or thirty years, what difference does it make if they have not been dealt with? Until they are dealt with my present is disturbed; unless they are acknowledged my present is disturbed and incomplete.

Fortunately I now know that there is something to remember, that there is an explanation. But this could so easily have not been the case. Were it not for events beyond my control, which pushed me into a recognition of my own state, I do not believe I would have been able to change. I might have gone to my grave a Doppelgänger.

STEVE WILLIAMS

1. Doppelgänger: a creature of German folklore, a "duplicate walker." It is the wraith or ghost of a living person and its appearance portends the madness and death of that person. However, it seems to me that it is a rich metaphor of more real disassociative states and offers the possibility of rediscovered life. (The legend of the vampire too can be seen as a dreamer's paradigm of half-remembered sexual abuse which has been woken in the Gothic castles of Transylvania.)

# Can you hear me?

The contributions to this chapter focus upon silences, telling about abuse, confrontations and being heard on our own terms which for many of us are central to making sense of child sexual abuse and its aftermath.

Silence is a particularly powerful motif of child sexual abuse. Silence is enforced upon us both by our abusers and by a society that at first *could* not listen, and now *will* not listen, to our experiences in *our own terms*. "Silence is golden?" and "The Dontell," together capture many of the issues that relate to the silences of sexual abuse.

Turning now to the vexing issue of "telling," the decision about whether and to whom and how to tell about sexual abuse has been tackled in various ways by the authors of this chapter, many of whom weigh up the need to be heard against the pressure to be silent. In contrast to Angie, in "Throat," who urges herself, and us, not to disclose abuse, some of the authors describe the difficulties involved in the "mechanics" of the actual telling. "Sit them down with a bottle" describes the difficulty of finding the right moment, place or words to tell about abuse; the author ends on a note that is echoed by Jan Chapple in her poem, "Oh life," which defiantly states that we should not only tell but we should also "go and give them hell."

We have also included accounts of confronting the abuser. While speaking out is described by many as both therapeutic and empowering, a number of the authors also depict the pain and loss that is often involved. "Confrontation" captures the parallel tracks of winning and losing in this context. Emma Bennett's experience,

96

however, was entirely different. Through her diary entry we learn of the tremendous support that she received from her family when they accompanied her to confront her grandfather. Emma saw the event as being "a wedding, a funeral and a rebirth all at once."

Finally, not all of the confrontations here refer to those between the abuser and abused; they also reflect the confrontations we have with ourselves, with therapists and with society itself, all of which further underline our need to be heard on our own terms.

---

## Silence is golden?

Snow falls silently,
Pauses then disappears.
It is a valuable,
Reflective time.
A chance to look inward,
For a journey of discovery.

Yet some things need to be said,
Not oppressed without speech.
I needed to tell—to yell!
Not find myself threatened,
Voiceless, I feel powerless.
Is silence so golden?

ANONYMOUS

## Throat

Throat, throat
Hold on tight
Don't scream
Or he might . . .

ANGIE

## Can you hear me?

Can you hear me?
Can you hear me calling?
Broken windows.
Lonely. So lonely!!
Human kindness??? Where is it?
I think it's going to rain today.

Broken windows.
I am the prisoner looking out through the
fragmented cracked pieces.
Sexually abused, you ask?
I ask the experts
But they can't tell me.
How can I tell them or anyone?
Can you hear me?

How does a two-year-old tell?
How does a five-year-old tell?
Where do little children go?

Where is safety when they are stolen and then abandoned?
Tell me how do I tell you I was sexually abused?

Can you hear me?

My memories belong to a two-year-old.
What does anyone remember when they are
two years old?

Does a two-year-old scream out in terror,
in pain when they hardly have the words
to speak?

When this child spoke—no one heard.
No one was there!
Tell me how do I prove it to you when I
can't prove it?

I have memories, two-year-old memories.
My body has evidence of that.

Can you hear me?

Someone walked away with my soul.
They robbed my spirit.
They murdered it. They tried! But, I was still alive.
I survived.

Can you hear me?

I ask the experts???
Some know. Some don't
Some don't know anything!!!

The survivors know.
They see it
They know it.
They experience it!!!

Can you hear me?

The deep spiritual wounding is so evident.
Why can't I believe myself?
Why can't I trust myself?
Why do I need validation from the
outside?

A two-year-old child, a five-year-old
child were sexually abused.
They have memories, as much as a two-year-
old and five-year-old could have!

How do I tell you?

How do I prove it?

Can you hear me?

No one will support me with the evidence.
My body does.
My feelings do.
My process tells me.
But, how do I tell?
How do I tell anyone?
Little children don't tell.
Mine belong to a secret place.

VALERIE GODFREY

## The Dontell

The Dontell
Came to live
In me

When I was
Very little
Only three.

The Dontell
Had for me
Great power
That took
Me over
Hour by hour.

The Dontell
Made me so
I couldn't tell
Inside
I had
To scream and yell.

The Dontell
Always was
Around
He made sure
my voice
I never found.

The Dontell stayed
And stayed
with me
Until
He shrank
By one degree.

The Dontell
Was scared
And on the run
But he'd fight

To stop me
Having fun.

The Dontell
Hard and hard
He fought
To stop
Me telling
Like I ought.

The Dontell
Getting
Smaller still
Cursed and spat
And wished
Me ill.

The Dontell's
On the run
You know
Allowing me
To grow
And grow.
The Dontell
Knows
He's for the floor
He's fighting hard
For one hold
More.

The Dontell's
Getting
Thin and frail
His roar's
Become
A tiny wail.

The Dontell's
Wail
Becomes a scream
That's all
He is—
A ghastly dream.

The Dontell
For me,
Is no more
I'm striding
Free
Out through the door.

Out through the door
And into the sun
Where I am
Free
To walk and run.

To walk and run
To sing and dance
Life holds
For me
A second chance!

ANGIE

*"The Dontell" (Don't Tell) was the monster who silenced me so I couldn't tell anyone what was happening to me.*

## Fact and fiction

TO ALL AND SUNDRY,
FROM MONDAY TO SUNDAY
KARK CLENT WAS
A REGULAR YOUNG GUY,
BUT WHEN DAY DIED TO NIGHT
AND CRIME DID IGNITE
KARK CLENT WAS
AN ABUSED YOUNG BOY,
HOW REAL WERE YOU THEN, SUPERMAN?

RICHIE B.

---

Glazed eyes fixed on the bedroom wall,
knees pressed tightly against the chipwood
my body lies motionless.
My brain is numb
locked in disbelief
his footsteps grow silent.
My eyes go back to the ceiling,
back to the spot where I had been
        I don't understand
        I'm a bad girl.
My mouth and throat hurt,
tears slide down my face
into my ears.
I bite my lip to stop my
self making a noise.
I must be quiet or Mum
will be angry.
Something shrivels
inside me and dies.

BERNIE

## Words

I am full of words.
They flow from me
Like a river.
A torrent of emotion,
Rushing headlong
Down a steep valley.
Echoing their message
For all to see.
Yet they do not heal my pain,
They do not ease my burden of guilt.
It cannot be written away,
I must live with it.
I write words
That no one can understand.
They sit and stare,
And try to know
What I am saying.
But my message is hidden
Deep inside,
Protected by meaningless words.
My madness
Threatens to overcome my life,
And I will be thrown into
A never-ending pit of confusion.
Tumbling over and over,
Unable to grasp the sanity
That means life.
Confusion rains down upon me,
Like drops of molten lead.
Covering and destroying.
Holding me within it,
To lie there,
Forever frozen in time.
Condemned never to know peace,

Held captive by my thoughts.
I watch, as the world turns,
Showing me what could have been.
A howl of rage erupts from within,
As I search for words.
My search is in vain,
For words cannot tell you
The agony I feel.
The ever present ache of despair,
The sadness which overwhelms.
They cannot describe
The ever growing longing and need.
The need for truth and forgiveness,
Which can never be met.

BETH (2)


## Sit them down with a bottle

Sit them down with a bottle
at their side?
Out for a walk on a warm
summer's evening?
Just after dinner, before,
or with coffee?
Serve the words on a plate?
In a bottle?
In neon lights across
their door?
In their home, in mine?
In a bar?
How do you tell the secret
to parents?
No one prepares you for this, or that
The words aren't important, it's the telling!

SHONA BREMNER

---

Since remembering the abuse I now know I am no oddball at all, I am perfectly sane. But I have changed, not in the ways I expected to change though. I expected my determined, strong side of my personality to disappear. I expected to become extremely dependent. Instead, I have both of these facets intact constantly. If it were not for my resilient side I would have "thrown in the towel" months ago— but instead I keep on and on. It is the resilient side to me which helped me to confront my parents recently—just six short months after I began to remember the abuse. I find that astounding to say the least. Although the confrontation was the most difficult thing I have ever had to do—I am pleased I have done it. I am pleased because seeing and experiencing their violent reaction has made me feel and believe the abuse did happen. Previously I had recurrent doubts— now I do not. Alright, so I have lost a brother to them—that is his problem now. He has also lost a kind, thoughtful sister who would have always been there for him. It has split the whole family apart— but I do not need to pretend any more.

MAGRYL

## Diary of the week leading up to the confrontation of my abuser with the truth
### or
## Monday 21 March 1994—Spring equinox— an important turning point in the year

My partner away in Devon attending a job interview as we are hoping/trying to move to a greener part of the land *soon*.

Feeling pressurized and anxious about that. Took my daughter (aged three) to nursery in the afternoon—sat in a café trying to focus my thoughts on the days ahead . . .

Paying bills and sorting out paperwork.

Partner returns home still not knowing if he has the job.

I go out to rehearsal for tomorrow's big concert with the orchestra in the cathedral. I play the French horn and have the famous

solo in Tchaikovsky's Fifth Symphony (slow movement) . . . nervous.
I've increased the ginseng capsules to two a day!

Came home—he hasn't got the job, but was in the last three
(out of forty-two applicants). Good but not good enough, he says!

*Tuesday 22 March*
Concert this evening on my mind all day. I also have my last counselling session before the big day on Saturday. A lot of pressure and
nerves. Wanting to really make the most of my session; to stay present, to feel, yet scared that if I do I'll be in no state to cope with the
concert. I cycle over, having left my daughter with friends, and in the
session I manage to explore all the above fears, and I *do* feel and cry
as I practice reading out the statement I have prepared for the confrontation with Grandad, who sexually abused me when I was a child.

And I was able to feel and express the pain, *and* be all right
again. I've come a long way!

Very nervous for the concert and big solo, but I stayed calm and
centered and played it the best I ever have! A major milestone for me:
to feel secure enough to express the music. It's also a very meaningful
solo to me, with personal associations to lost love, lost family—a kind
of deep yearning, mourning, farewell, yet also an affirmation of love.

*Wednesday 23 March*
Awoke after only five hours' sleep—a wild and windy night. Feeling
on a bit of a high after the concert still. Drove with my daughter to
visit my sister in Devon on her twenty-fifth birthday. Another major
event for me, undertaking a solo trip on big fast motorways.

Lovely to be with my sister. She's written a beautiful story all
about the need to live *real* life, as in "the *real* world is whatever makes
us happy." Very inspiring. We went for tea, and danced about the
cathedral close throwing magnolia petals up against the blue evening
sky and nearly full moon.

*Thursday 24 March*
Little sleep, again. My daughter (and me) a bit stressed-out at being
away from home—our relationship stretched and tetchy. Go for a

swim, with nutty pool attendants trying out all the different wave and fountain functions seemingly at random—get hysterical!

Had an exhausted lunch back at sister's flat, then drove the two hours home.

*Friday 25 March*
A day of nitty-gritty preparation. Sorting out the house, the bills, the cat, and packing and gathering everything up.

Partner's last day of term—he arrives home and eventually we leave, arriving at my mum's house, my childhood home, for supper.

Gathered there are my mum, my sister, and her boyfriend, my brother and his girlfriend, and us three.

It feels good to arrive, but a lot of apprehension. All the plans and complexities, hopes and fears—how's it all going to work out? Unknown, with unknown consequences.

The first unexpected thing is that when Mum rang Grandad (he has been living on the other side of the village since about 1982-3) to say I wanted to "pop round on Saturday morning," my other sister (who at the time still had a relationship with him) was there. So she became involved sooner rather than later, which in fact did much to clear the air between us.

The evening wore on, and the moment for discussing the next day could not be delayed any more.

We all sat down in the big room (interestingly, no "couples" sat together). I explained what I wanted to happen and why. (I hadn't seen Grandad for eleven years or so.)

I wanted to confront Grandad with the truth of what he did to me, and to have it witnessed, here and now, in the present, by my family. To bring the deep, dark secret out into the light—so that the denial of it all through my childhood would somehow be ended. For him to know that my family *believe me*. To make/seek reparation . . . wanting reparation.

My brother being defensive, and making me justify myself. "Do you want to totally destroy him?" No—that's not my reason—his reactions are irrelevant, I'm doing this for *me*. I want the truth witnessed in the present.

At one point I was talking about how Grandad used to masturbate his second wife on the sofa, under a rug, while watching TV—with us in the room—that I was very aware of this, sometimes sitting on the other side of him . . .

My brother said "He used to do that with me too, but I never thought anything of it." Me: "Well, I *do* think something of it." Mum and I having a hug: "We're all with you."

My sister getting angry: "Look, if this is what Emma needs to do, let's just bloody help her do it."

Then my brother started to cry—admitting his pain for the first time, perhaps. I went over to him and we had a big cry together.

"Tears are good," I said. "We couldn't cry when we needed to."

Then *everyone* was crying (except my partner). We were all acknowledging the pain together—the first time that has *ever* happened. Admitting that we are connected; we are a family; we went through something together. Not even at Mum and Dad's separation was there any shared grief.

By this point I had decided that even if we couldn't get in through Grandad's door (because he was ill or his wife was too obstructive, as had been threatened), then I would read my statement on the doorstep with everyone around me. By now the fear of it "not happening" was less, since already so much had moved for the better.

That was the beginning of the miracle. I was awake until 3 a.m. working out the words of my statement and reducing it to 30 seconds (my partner timing it!). I wanted it to be quick enough not to give Grandad any reaction time, yet to say everything I needed to say, so if he did die immediately afterwards, would I have said everything I ever wanted?

Three hours' sleep.

*Saturday 26 March*
A fantastic sunny blue sky, perfect warm day.

Cherry blossom in the garden.

We were all preparing in our different ways. I went around taking photos of flowers, and my books, and my good luck fish present from Mum.

I bathed with essences of lavender, geranium, lemon and ylang-ylang. Put on my jeans and big brown boots—feet firmly in the ground, in the mud—earthed. And my fiery colored top and my jewels and my black jacket.

Couldn't eat. Drank nettle tea and picked garden flowers for Grandma's grave (in the village churchyard). Flowers for remembrance. Her favorite, forget-me-not. She was my witness in a sense from all that time ago, for she spoke the words to Dad, and he didn't understand, didn't act. "I hope he's not interfering with her."

Dad arrived, a big event in itself, Mum and Dad being "together" for the first time in years—and we all assembled. I went to the loo (again!), and did a breathing exercise to calm down. Felt in my pockets for my lucky charms, and my piece of paper—and we set off.

The Magnificent Seven, we set off down the road—we felt like an army—more like seventy—our feet sounding on the road, united, together, me supported. Time in slow motion—the longest short walk of my life. We walked in a loop so as to approach his house from the side and give him no warning.

About halfway round, Mum and Dad were both suddenly supporting me, holding me, one on either side.

Felt *so* amazing. A miracle. I was crying (even my fantasies didn't come up to this). Mum: "Do you want to stop?" Me: "No, keep going. It's just so incredible."

*Reparation*

Head up, smiling, sure. Struggling, but knowing I had the strength to do it, that I *had* to do it.

As we walked near to my old primary school, a gang of people were digging up the road. The symbolism struck me—of the digging, digging up of the old road.

Dad and the two partners went off and loitered tactically behind the garages, so as not to be seen. Dad had given me a whistle which I had in my pocket and would blow if I needed them!

My brother, sister, mother and I went to knock on Grandad's door; his wife opened it and was smiling tensely. "You have visitors," she called out. We went in. Grandad came out of the kitchen looking confused. His presence gave me no physical shock—he was the same, just older. He was stooped, with a fat stomach, bent over, with watery eyes and thick glasses. He kept pointing with long fingers, being bombastic, mocking, trying to control and direct the situation— but he couldn't. There was no way I was going to let him.

"Who's this then? Who's that? That's not Emma? You're not Emma?"

So I replied, looking straight at him:

"Yes, I'm Emma."

I felt centered and focused on what I had come to do.

He tried to maneuver us into a room, but we decided to simply do it in the hall, all of us standing up, me opposite him.

"I'm surrounded," he said. The words of an ex-soldier, finally admitting defeat.

Then I read out my statement:

"I've got something very important to say to you. It's the truth. From when I was nine you deliberately and consciously sexually abused me. You put your fingers in my vagina and you masturbated me. This is not an act open to misinterpretation. You as the adult were and always will be responsible.

"You damaged me deeply. Your secret is out. I have told a lot of people and they believe me."

I look at him, and calmly continue, despite his intakes of breath, grunts, and attempts to interrupt. He looks terrified, accepting of the truth. Confronted with it he makes no attempt to deny it, this time, spoken directly by me, to him. It's as if his whole posture and being was accepting that this was the truth.

I turn away and walk towards the front door, a sea of voices behind me saying "We believe Emma"—undoing the catch in slow motion—walking out, upright, calm, dignified. My partner came towards me and we hugged, me crying, saying over and over "I did it." Mum followed, crying, hugging: "He admitted it, he admitted it, Darling." He said, "Ok, I accept that . . ." Mum and my brother both heard him say that, as I was leaving.

We were all crying on and off—tears of vast relief, catharsis. We all went to the churchyard where Grandma is buried. Her tombstone reads "Just Jane," which had become very meaningful to me, as in "Justice." I put my flowers and message on her grave, with Dad. I felt anger at Grandad and pain for myself, and for all women down the ages whose lives have been shattered. I also felt relief and release. A very strong sense of the spiritual, of the rightness of Justice—of something very powerful at work. That ultimately everything we do comes back to us. That we are all responsible for our own actions.

Surrounded and supported by my family, I went home, passing the new road now being laid.

"You are so strong, so brave, you made it happen." Everyone telling me in different ways.

We drank hot sweet tea in the garden, and everyone drew, painted and stuck things on to a big banner for me—I provided an old sheet to form this commemorative banner—I wanted something tangible to keep from this day—it is a miracle in itself, a real treasure!

I felt a hundred years younger!

Later we danced, and went to the pub and shouted out in freedom at the beautiful full moon. A feeling of light, lightness; of being in a new continent.

"You've come to join the rest of us. Welcome," said Mum.

The first time ever as a family we've carried out a ritual. It felt like a wedding, a funeral and a rebirth all at once. As if everything came to a most incredible resolution; reclamation, reparation.

I went through the door in '94—I stepped through the fear, and Grandad has no power over me now.

A great coming together.

*26 April 1994: One month on*
After the euphoria, coming down. After the operation, needing a time of convalescence (almost impossible to get!). Needing to go within and digest, and slowly admitting and accepting that *I am*

*everything* that has ever happened to me—that becoming fully whole from this new place will be exciting, transforming and difficult.

EMMA BENNETT

## Why do I feel so blue?

Towards the end of the day, my mind is in turmoil. What will happen in court? What is going to be thrown at me? I wonder whether I should tell my parents how I feel? No—best not to, I've upset them enough at the moment. Poor Dad, he's the one I took all my anger out on, yet I look at him, now that he knows what I went through, I can see under his outside attitude that he's ok, he's really broken by the fact that some man (bastard) made his child do sexual acts with him. Dad won't talk about it at the moment. It's my fault as I should have told him what was going on.

Memories keep flooding back of what happened. Sometimes it's just a sentence or a scene from a TV program that triggers it off. I shut myself off from the real world and go into a world of my own. That world I hate being in, but I just flitter into it. I come out of it eventually—usually feeling down.

Mum is good to me. She now knows all that happened. She seems to be ok, she asks about different events that took place—she ends up angry about it. Should I talk to her when she asks or not? I don't know. I feel like running away—I'll change my identity then no one will know me, no one will know my past—a new life.

No—I'd miss all my friends and family. Thought about suicide again—at least I'd be gone—I'm sure that would please a lot of people.

But—why should I give up my life when I have a lot to offer? I don't know. I wish I could feel better inside—perhaps when court is over my world will change. Should I not get the result I want—what do I do? Go after the person involved? Do I hurt him as he did me? Do I kill him—maim him? I don't know.

I have a lot going on in my mind. Perhaps that's why I'm so blue. Hope it changes soon. I'd prefer to have some color back in my world. It'll be great when I can go to sleep to actually sleep well without any worries about different aspects of the court.

Why do I feel so blue? Because some bastard has ruined my life to date. As soon as he's sorted out, then, hopefully, my world will feel worth living for.

WAYNE SMITH

*Written by a 25-year-old man after five months of therapy*

---

*To this day I still cannot believe that I not only "lost" my mother at disclosure some three years ago, but that she probably would have treated me just as badly if I'd disclosed at the age of ten. I survived, but the price I paid is almost unthinkable.*

*"Night cry" no longer applied (I think) because the last line (in Latvian) says, in effect, "I will wait for you for ever," but I've stopped waiting—it is too painful.*

## Night cry

Mother of my dreams, take flight and come to me like a seagull swoops across a sky fractured with clouds.

Mother of my desires, let this dream called Hope clasp me in its godly arms like a womb clutches its unborn.

Mother of my pain, remember the child that you are within the child that I am bursting to break free.

Mother of my joy, come out of the haunting past that beckons in my brief moments of lucidity.

Mother of mothers, like a wolf I howl to a moon and a dream that refuses to heed my soul call.

Mamma, mana mamma, *es tevi gaidu un gaidu un gaidu.*

OLGA CHEN

## Extract from a letter written to a dad who abused his daughter when she was fourteen

Dear Dad,

I think it's time I sat down and wrote this to you. If only you knew the full extent of guilt and pain I am going through now. It would probably have been better if I had written this letter earlier—or even had the courage to say "no"—but I didn't.

If you knew how dirty I feel, and how many lies I had to tell when I was younger about what was happening. I always wonder why you picked on me—but I suppose I will never know.

Do you know that as a little girl I felt unloved? You always seemed to leave me out and care for others. Then all of a sudden you were buying things for me, but they were for the wrong reasons, weren't they?

Do you know what it's like not knowing if your daughter belongs to your dad or your husband? I'm sorry to say I would need proof of your operation to believe she's not yours. Although Mum was still alive when the attacks on me first took place, you knew I wouldn't say anything because it would probably have killed her.

Do you know I can't stand anyone—even the children—to cuddle me because of what's happened. That's why the kids are having problems—because I can't love them properly. I wish things could have been different. I wish you had loved me as your daughter, and not for what I had to offer. If we had had a proper relationship—

more like father and daughter than lovers—I would not be so suspi-
cious of men in general.

Well, I hope you stay well and healthy. I love you now and always, despite what happened. If you can still look me in the eye and
talk about what happened, then it's your move. If I don't hear from
you I will know.

Love,

ANGELA WILLIAMS

## To Dad

Dad I hope you understand,
By telling the truth I hurt your pride.
Each day I think of your pitiful face,
Living in your far-off land.

Please help me to help you.
Help me to love, the way daughters do.
Give me your shoulder to cry on,
And a hankie to dry my eyes on.

Dad, I'm doing this for both of us;
I'm not creating or making a fuss.
I love you dearly.
Don't worry—we'll come out of it.

And one day we'll look back
To this time now,
Laugh and giggle
The way father and daughter do.

"S."

## Addition

I forgot what I was trying to lead up to.

I did all this writing and separating of him and me so that I could do something really difficult for me. That was to write him out of my life. I needed Nancy around as a kind of anchor although she was really worried about me and I was doing all this on my own initiative. I had to trust myself and had selected the day when I became 32½ as the day to do it (11 November 1993). It put a lot of pressure on me, but it also helped as I called that day the barrier and wanted to have it all down by then. This was so I could write to him.

I chose a card with a gorilla on the front with BOLLOCKS printed on it. Inside I called all I had written his unnatural stuff and I put a simple message inside saying I was returning all his shit to him and I was no longer part of his life, nor he mine.

I didn't want to include any of my emotions or thoughts other than this, as I feel he just didn't deserve that at all.

This was very difficult and I mailed it that day. I then wrote to my mum, who still lives with him because she loves him. I said I didn't want to cut her out of my life, that I had to do this and that if he would only stop lying, face his truth and get help, even he could find a way out. This was for myself as I didn't want to do such a violent act out of pure revenge for my own sake. I wanted it to have some purpose.

I understand that he tried to kill himself after my card, but he and Mum went to see the Samaritans and he is now getting counselling because he does not want to do this to other children.

This has been my only aim regarding him—to stop his abuse— but I do not want to take responsibility for that. I just don't care. It's also why I've changed my name by deed pole to Wendar, to break *any* connection with him.

Since then I've still worked with Nancy trying to sort out my feelings, etc., and also regarding my mother, who I'm not sure what to feel about. I know in a way she did her best to help us survive and this was highlighted recently when I went to a gender studies talk given by a lady who had survived ritual abuse. According to her, most murders happen when the wife leaves or is about to leave. Also

Nancy said that a lot of the cases of fathers killing families and then themselves were very likely because the secret of their abusive behavior was about to be revealed.

That's why I think I identified, as an individual, with *Schindler's List*. That constant fear of death and the power of the abuser (power in its negative sense). The constant need to please the abuser and pretend nothing was happening, that we weren't afraid or angry, ever. It doesn't relate on the societal level, but then again I think male violence probably does.

KEVIN WENDAR

———————

In 1990 I attended a group—it was hard, really hard—and I lost my eleven-year-old son through it. He no longer lives with me and hasn't since I went to the group. He is fourteen years old now and lives with his grandparents. I also lost contact with my younger brother because of being honest, bringing things out into the open. For three years he hasn't spoken to me.

WAS IT WORTH IT? I used to wonder but now I know it was. I discovered the real me. I'm just as good as anyone, nobody has the right to treat me badly, and even though I'm fat, someone still loves me.

JEAN CAZAUX

———————

I don't remember much about my early childhood except that Mum was never around much, so Dad was always the one to mind us. That was fine with me. He never shouted; Mum yelled all the time. He never smacked us; Mum would beat us for the smallest thing. Dad gave us sweets and money; Mum barely gave us the time of day. So it seemed quite natural always to be sat on Dad's knee or cuddled up in bed next to him.

I thought that he was a natural, loving father until the day came when he cuddled me a bit more tightly and kissed me a bit more wetly. Then he lay on top of me and tried to have sex with me. I was "lucky," if that's the right word, when I told him to stop because it hurt. He did stop. I was only about five years old then, and as far as I can remember he didn't do it again.

Mum and Dad got divorced when I was six and he left home. We'd see him at weekends and it would break my heart when he'd go. I'd watch him from my bedroom window until he was out of sight. For years I buried that incident at the very back of my mind, then at about fourteen years old I started to experiment with sex with my boyfriend and it all came back to me. I didn't want to believe it. I loved my dad and I'd never seen him hurt a fly, so how could he have done that to me? Although he did have some strange habits, like picking up old combs and handkerchiefs off the pavements and keeping them. Once again I forced my memories to the back of my mind. They made me feel uncomfortable and I had never told anyone about it. They stayed hidden for about another thirteen years, then something happened and out came the old skeletons.

I'd married in 1982 and all through my marriage there had been periods when Dad had stayed with us. I had a child in 1985, a boy. Dad was chuffed to mintballs and was a perfect Grandad. Always happy to look after Steve when he was a baby, take him out on his bike when he was big enough to ride one, take him to infants school when he started there and babysit at night if we wanted to go out. Sometimes when Dad went back to his second family in Wales he would even take Steven with him to "give us some time to ourselves."

In 1989 my marriage broke up and I was devastated. I had to get away, so I packed a bag and Steve and I got on a train to Wales. I was only five minutes from my stepmother's house, Steve had been happily chatting all the way, when suddenly he said "Grandad tried to put his willy up my bum." I felt anger, sickness and disgust inside but on the outside I pretended that I'd not heard him properly and asked him to say it again clearly. He repeated the same words exactly. I tried to look complacent about it (even though my face was burning) and asked him, "Didn't it hurt?" He said, "No, it was soft and squishy," and giggled. I told him that it was a very strange thing to do but not to worry about it.

We changed the subject and arrived at our destination. It was two hours before I could get my dad alone. I made him come for a walk on the beach with me. How could I say anything in front of his wife and daughters? When we got to the beach I told him exactly what my son had said and asked him did he do it. He denied it emphatically and said that I should question Steve about it more closely. I told him no way, that I didn't want Steve to remember it ever again and said that I'd got enough childhood memories of my own, thank you. He didn't comment on that but said that Steve must have seen it on TV or on a video, which is impossible because they don't show such explicit stuff on TV and I've never had a pornographic video in the house. Steve was four years old. I told my dad that he was *never* to be alone near Steve again and that if there was a hint of anything else I would call the police, but of course I had no proof or physical evidence. The other problem was that although I hated my dad for what he'd done I also still loved him, though God knows why.

After this I spoke to my brother and sister about our childhood. My brother swears Dad never touched him sexually, but I have found out that when my sister was about five years old he was sitting her on his knee and getting her to masturbate him.

After a few months I returned to Wales and I went to the pub with my seventeen-year-old stepsister. Jolene and I had quite a few drinks, we were laughing and joking when she said Fred (our dad) was a dirty old pervert. Alarm bells rang in my head and I asked her why she said that. She said that he just gave her the creeps. That was when I decided to tell her what had happened to me and Steve. Naturally she was horrified and very upset. What worried her the most was that Fred would spend hours at night reading to Anna (my eight-year-old stepsister) alone in her room. She said that he'd never touched her but that she was going to keep an eye on him. I did and I didn't want to tell her, if you know what I mean. I know how heavy this secret can be to carry round.

Several years passed since Steve's allegation and gradually Dad wheedled his way back into my life. Steve was always closely watched with him, and Jessie (my little girl) was only left in his care if it was absolutely necessary. Dad went back to Wales last summer, which was a relief as he'd got a flat in Manchester by now that was only ten minutes away and Steve was always asking to go round there and I was always having to make up some excuse or other why he couldn't go. Also I'd told my fiancé everything. He'd become curious about why I always watched Steve like a hawk and when I explained he wasn't very happy about it, to say the least.

It was only one week after Dad had gone when Jessie turned round and out of the blue said "Grandad weed on me." I gradually coaxed out of her more information and found out that it had happened in a bedroom and that the "wee" went all over her tummy. The only explanation I could come up with for this is that Fred had masturbated over her. Jessie was only three years old. Fred phoned me two days later and again I confronted him. Of course he denied it. He said, "She must have made it up." How many three-year-olds do you know that could make up something like that?

I've now told my dad that I never want to see him again and that the only contact that I will have with him is on the telephone to sort out his catalogue payments. My sister hasn't spoken to him in about ten years and never will again. She says she wishes he were dead. My brother doesn't speak to him now either, since hearing about Jessie. Shortly after I told Dad what Jessie had said, he sent me the key to his flat to return to the council. He's decided not to return to Manchester. I went to his flat with my cousin. I'd told her how weird he was and she wanted a look around. In there were his usual collection of old combs and hankies, but also a large bag of ladies' knickers, tights, bras, silk scarves and about forty odd gloves (presumably used for masturbation). I told him when he next phoned that I'd seen these things, that he made me sick and that he needs psychiatric help.

But what worries me now is that Katie (my eighteen-year-old stepsister) had a baby girl six months ago. What happens in three years' time? Will Kaylie be talking about things that she supposedly "saw on TV" or will she be "making things up"? Is it over now or will he continue down the line? My kids are aged four and nine now and are healthy and happy. They've had it gently drummed into them that it is not right for people to touch their "private parts" and they understand and trust me enough to tell me if anything "untoward" happens, even if it happens accidentally during a game. I wish that I could have trusted my mum, then maybe he'd have been stopped years ago.

LYNDA WILL

## Brotherly love

Two and a half years ago
you said you'd ring back.
Last Saturday, you did.
Fortunately, I wasn't in—
so the decision to speak or not
to speak was taken from me.
I'd had much to say to you . . .
I'd written you a letter full of my pain.

You said, trying to be brotherly
and failing, "It wasn't that bad,"
admirably ignoring your hurt and mine.
I question this shared history.
I tried to explain how I felt.
You didn't even think to listen
patiently. As my older sibling
how could you be other than correct?
How could you remember other than perfectly?

I consider the power of your memory,
pitted against mine.
Survival, like a collapsed bridge between us.
Two and a half years ago
you, leading the charge of "The Family,"
questioned my sense and my sanity

and I was too close to rage
to hear how you called me
a liar by any other name.
Then, for the first time—ever—
I refused to pretend we were all fine,
I refused to play the game.
And today, though you fish for
trivialities—I'm still the same.

I thought we had a relationship
worth saving. But silence has taught
me how truth lies within.
Time is no great healer of mine.
Only words, only communication—
but talking can come too late.
When we're between a rock and a hard place;
Truth changes everything.

MANDY PRECIOUS


## Oh life

Oh life, my life
When will you be kind
When will you afford me
True peace of mind

Cheer up—chin out
Things could be worse
At least you've now found
The meaning of verse

Oh heart, my heart
Much feeling you hold

Who'd ever have thought
You could be so bold

So much pain and misery
They thought you'd never tell
Rise undisturbed and simply
GO AND GIVE THEM HELL!!

JAN CHAPPLE (NÉE DURKIN)


## Confrontation

As you walk in the room
My flesh crawls,
To see your slimey smile
And hear your false voice.
You are hiding,
God are you hiding,
Behind your powerful suit
And expensive life.
But I can see through you,
Find your weaknesses
And gain my power.

And so the battle begins,
Words flying around the room
Aimed at my heart,
Designed to pierce
And kill.

But I do not die,
I do not give up,
No way.
My words are as good as yours,

And I have the ultimate weapon on my side,
I have the truth.

And through showing you the truth
I am faced with my worst fears,
As like a snake shedding its skin
You come out from behind your mask,
And show your true colors.
God you do not care,—
You do not care for me
For my feelings.
All you think about is yourself,
Your life,
Your reputation,
Your image.
You panic and run
Scattering your accusations,
Treading on the people below you,
Trampling and wounding them
In your effort to escape.

And as you dismiss
Everything I say.
And attack my words and deeds,
Looking at me
As if I am crazy,
Telling me I am selfish, cruel, ungrateful,
I stand taller.
I know you will not win.
And I take a deep breath
And tell you.
I remember.
I know.
I believe.

And sitting there before me
You stare with horror,
And laugh at me,
Throwing your hands in the air.
How could your daughter
Betray you so?
I have not betrayed you.
I did not even want to hurt you.
But it is my turn now
To reclaim my life,
To acknowledge the past,
To find my freedom.

And as you leave,
Hurriedly, with hardly a backward glance,
I know I have won,—
I have told you
And faced you
And not given in.

Yet as the pain returns to my body,
I know that I have also lost,—
That my father is gone,
That my family are gone.
And I am left in this room
Chasing shadows in the darkness
Alone.

PENNY K.

# Turned on a tide

"Turned on a tide" is a short chapter about transition and change. It also represents the precursors of, and the opportunities for, change. As with all change, there will always be an element of loss which is captured in many of the pieces and very often the place to which we move is not a certain one: it may be into healing, as Athena depicts in "Metamorphosis," or the place we arrive at may be unknown. Andrew Ravensdale describes one such journey into the unknown in "Trees, water, stone," where he attempts to retrieve and confront buried memories.

## Add up

Sad
Bad
Had a
Grandad
Mad man
Glad man
Dad's dad man
Gradually

A dead man
   Bladder problems
   Sadder problems
   Glad of his problems
Threading
Unclad naked piecing
   Wads of
   Sad
   Bad together
   Gradually
   Adding up

HEATHER MCEWAN-LENNOX

## Trees, water, stone

I didn't know what I was looking for until I found it. I'd forgotten it existed. And the night before, I hadn't thought I was going anywhere at all.

I woke for the second time, between first light and sunrise, to hear the rising tide against the rocks. From the cleft where I lay on the sand in my sleeping bag, I could see the surf rolling up the beach. I wondered, for a minute, if I was passive enough to lie there and let the water cover me.

I decided I wasn't. I dragged myself to the top of the cliffs, and found the car. I could hardly sit upright, and I didn't want to fall asleep—I thought if I did I would be found, and I still wanted to die.

I drove, somehow, to Wadebridge. I didn't know why I was going. From the river, still half-stunned by the effect of the pills—the violence I had been doing to myself—I saw some trees, on a hill above the town.

I thought, "I want to go there."

On the way, I threw away my driving license. The last ID I had. I didn't want the old identity any more.

The wood—though I hadn't realized it at first—was at the top of Park Place. The street where my mother's house used to stand. I had been through Wadebridge on the way to the coast, and had discovered—though I couldn't have given directions, or drawn you a map—that I could still find the way.

The wood was mature, and the undergrowth was thick. It covered the slope of the hill, and the paths followed the contours. It was obviously the "magical wood" that I had been delighted with as a child, and could never locate in memory.

I found what amounted to a "den," among the bushes and the trees. I didn't know why I was choosing that particular place. I could hide there, and worry no one with my zombie-like state.

I curled up like a child, on the leaves, and lay there, half-dozing, half-stunned. I still thought—and hoped—I was going to die. When I stood, I vomited. Black bile, and the husks of the capsules I had swallowed.

For a while, I sat. With my back against a tree, facing uphill. As if I was afraid of slipping down. It isn't the orientation I would choose now. I like to see the land below me.

I realized I was sitting with my knees apart, cupping my genitals with my open hands, as if they were sore and swollen. They weren't. And then I remembered.

I had been there before. I had used to run out of the house, and hide there, when I was four years old. When I was too frightened—or too angry, or too ashamed—to stay at home.

Some phrases came to mind. "When I've been bad." "When the voices come." And then, less distinctly: "When I'm a man I'll stay out in the woods all night, and then I'll die."

Slowly, I began to realize I had been abused more often than the two or three discrete instances I remembered. It had lasted a whole season. From March to September.

By evening—somewhat to my disappointment—I still wasn't dead, or even in a coma. But I was very thirsty. I went in search of water. Intuitively, I knew there was water around.

I staggered to the top of the hill, avoiding the lovers, the strollers, the evening exercisers of overfed dogs. I didn't want anyone to see me, and I didn't want them to know there was anything wrong.

I found I was in Coronation Park, where my great-aunt used to take me, and where we used to sit on a bench and overlook the town. But the only water I found was a closed concrete cistern, and a horse-trough covered with slime.

Eventually, I stumbled back down the hill. I didn't know what I was going to do. And then, when I least expected it, I found a stream—at the bottom of the wood, across the road.

I knelt, and drank. Just enough to wet my lips. And another phrase returned to mind: "I drank a cup of water in my hand."

I made my way along the riverbank. There were some bushes, where I could lie out of sight of the road. As the night grew colder, I gathered up the straw that some spring flood had left. "Feathers," I thought. That was what I used to call bracken leaves, when I was a child.

I had been there, too. And I could recall, now, the precise incident. One night I had hidden in the woods too long, and when I got back my mother had locked me out. "I want to come in!" I shouted from the back yard. "I want my tea!"

"You can sleep in the coal-house!" she yelled. "You've been a bad boy!"

And that, I think, was the end of the abuse. But it was also a rejection, which—at that age—I thought was the end of the world.

The loss and abandonment I felt that night, as a four-year-old child, was the loss and abandonment I was feeling again, as a man of forty-five. And I wanted—as I had wanted then—to die.

Finally, the night was too cold for me. Even in September. I had on only a sweatshirt.

I staggered back along the road I had crossed, to reach the stream—heading, though I wasn't completely sure of it, back towards Wadebridge. And I remembered some more.

Going home, the next morning, with straws in my hair. My father worrying, my mother feigning incomprehension. Demanding boiled egg and "soldiers" for breakfast—what I would have had for my tea, the night before. And going with my father to show him where I'd been, and insisting—against his denials—that there really was a stream.

The road we walked back home on, against my initial protests that we were going the wrong way, was the road I was walking on that morning, forty years later. And as I remembered the child I had once been—I almost was that child again, for a while—my strongest sense was of not having been believed.

I drove, eventually, to Liskeard. It was, after all, my birthplace: "home." And isn't home the place where when you go there, they have to take you in? The GP wasn't impressed. He told me to get an address, and come back. I stumbled—almost by accident—on a decent little hotel, with a decent manager. He did take me in.

The next morning, I was exhausted. Almost sleepwalking. I became hyperconscious of other people's feelings. I felt I was in the way—a nuisance—and wandered off.

I found a playground, where I had once sat on a bench with one of my great-aunts, and watched the other children play. I couldn't have found it if I'd been trying. From there, I could see the cemetery that I had visited unsuccessfully a few days before. The one where my great-grandfather is buried.

From where I was sitting, I could see that here was one grave, isolated from all the rest. Out of sight of the gate. As if it lay in what had once been unconsecrated ground, reserved for suicides and felons.

I went. It was my great-grandfather's.

"Right, you bastard," I thought. "You *were* my mother's abuser."

I sat on the stone for a while, and smoked a cigarette. It felt superbly disrespectful.

ANDREW RAVENSDALE

J.K. HORN

## Metamorphosis

Metamorphosis
from the binding once
necessary cocoon of the
caterpillar past.

Struggling, fighting
through the birth-pangs of life
the Butterfly finally emerges.

Free to fly.

ATHENA

## My dad

Although I was fifteen when he came into my life, I can say I loved
and trusted him completely, once I got to know him properly. My
mum got remarried when I was sixteen. I can say now that I resented
my stepdad a little in the beginning. It wasn't really till I was seventeen that I accepted him as a dad. He brought stability into my life,
which was something that had been lacking. My dad cared a lot for
me, he provided for me and gave me what he could. But, the most important thing he gave me was his love.

He gave me away on my wedding day and I was so proud he was
my dad. He performed his part as though I was one of his own daughters.

I had my daughter when I was nineteen and the way my dad reacted when I was in labor, you would have thought it was his first
grandchild being born, not his thirteenth. He was so impatient, he
couldn't wait to see her. He was a great papa to her.

When he died a year ago at Christmas, I was so lost without him.
He died on 29 December 1992 at 5.30 p.m., from a massive heart attack.

At the funeral service my oldest brother tried to comfort me but
I couldn't let him get close. I got the comfort I needed from my aunt.

It took me ages to accept the fact that my dad was dead. It wasn't really till Christmas was approaching that I began to fret. I dreaded Christmas without him there. Life has not been the same since he died. I have lost the security I had. I miss him so much it still hurts. When I am feeling down I cry a little for him. He truly was My Dad and he loved me as much as I loved him.

It was through my dread of Christmas without Dad that I began to remember having been abused as a child. I realized my dad was no longer there to protect me from harm.

I'm glad he never knew what my brothers did to me as a child.

JOAN MARY SIMPSON

## Looking back

I am a survivor, assured and free at last!! An adult looking ahead, having fun and laughing, I look back to that frightened child, and all frightened children, with compassion, understanding and love.

An abbreviated account of my life would be as follows:

| | |
|---|---|
| 1947 | Born youngest of a family of five in a working-class northern environment, with loving but elderly parents. They were both forty when I was born and my father's health was deteriorating. |
| 1954 | The sexual abuse started on a regular basis. |
| 1957 | My eldest brother and sister discovered what was happening and placed the guilt with me. |
| 1958 | First attempt at suicide. |
| 1960 | First thoughts about my sexual orientation. |
| 1960–5 | Blackouts, etc., regular treatment by GP for depression and nervous problems. |
| 1962–4 | Sexual behavior with males—made me feel even more confused. |
| 1963 | Second attempt at suicide—wanted to be murdered, felt that was what I deserved. |

| | |
|---|---|
| 1966 | Tried to conform—became engaged. |
| 1967 | Married—for all the wrong *reasons*. |
| 1971 | No children—so decided to separate from my husband. |
| 1973 | Came out to myself about my lesbianism. |
| 1975 | Divorce finalized. |
| 1964–78 | Good progressive career with a scientific manufacturer working up from office junior to sales and for the last five years buyer/manager. |
| 1978–84 | Became full-time single carer, looking after both invalid parents. |
| 1980 | Commenced part-time study, in social sciences with the Open University. |
| 1984 | Left the north-east of England for a new start in Scotland. (This move was precipitated by the return of my brother, the abuser.) |
| 1984–5 | Various jobs at different levels of administration. |
| 1985 to present | Started a new career in social work, and now hold a senior post. |
| 1986 | My mother died and at last no longer have contact with my abuser—free of him at last. |
| 1988 | Graduated from the Open University with a BA (open) (in social sciences). |
| 1990 | Graduated from Queen's Glasgow with a diploma in domiciliary care management. |
| 1992 | Studying part-time with University of Dundee for Certificate in Community Care; CC1 and CC2 completed, CC3 to be completed. |
| 1993 | Following counselling, etc., disclosed my abuse to some close friends and relatives (cousins) and my line manager at work. |
| 1994 | My new life begins in earnest and I start to do the things I didn't do because of my childhood experiences. |

I know now I was not to blame, I am no longer afraid of the truth, I am stronger in many ways and proud to be me, a survivor!

HILDA SMITH

## My own home

At last the privacy of my own home
I close my eyes and breathe deeply
My hair is beginning to grey
My face is rather pale
No longer moving . . .
No longer running . . .
I can now make out those distortions
No noise . . .
No family . . .
No Mother looking at me . . .
Leaning heavily against the door
And fighting the urge to cry
I'd never done anything right before
And nearing forty now
I've suffered so much
These past few months
With memories flooding and taunting
An unloved thing may wither and wilt
But it needn't die . . . No, it needn't die
Changing life makes pain fade away
Here I have my own place
And in my own way
No . . . I won't cry
I almost died away to nothing
While deep, deep inside me
Despite all that I survived
Something moved
It stretched and it reached
A sense that I am now growing
I feel the warmth of sunshine all around
At peace to be myself
At last, the privacy of my own home . . .

JAN CHAPPLE (NÉE DURKIN)

## Bobby and Jenny

Bobby's been around for years and years
Jenny's just starting to cry her tears.
Bobby's arrogant tough but safe
Jenny's a victim a desperate waif.

Bobby is a barbed-wire fence, a twelve-mile exclusion zone
Jenny's weeping in the corner, loathing her body.
Bobby is competitive, aggressive and angry
Jenny's a "yes" girl, but permanently hungry for love.
Jenny is Grandad's girl, the one who chose to play his games.
Bobby came out so her parents wouldn't guess his aims.

Jenny went to school and got kicked and burned
Bobby fought back and got reported.
Jenny hates Bobby for his big mouth, uncouth words, and
    permanent one-upmanship
Bobby despises Jenny for her need to keep everyone calm and
    everything safe.

Bobby has never been big enough to protect Jenny
Jenny has never been clever enough to protect herself.

When Jenny is on the outside Bobby is kicking out hard
Don't let them do that! Fight back!
When Bobby is on the outside everyone is kept so far at bay, no
    one can see Jenny.

Bobby wants to kick the shit out of everyone
    who comes too close.
Jenny wants to burn the shit out of herself for
    wanting people to come so close.
Bobby comes out at work and to greet my family
Jenny can be coaxed out by very close friends.

I dream of Bobby and Jenny co-existing peacefully
    of them liking each other
I dream of Bobby and Jenny merging to form one
    whole person.
I want Jenny on the outside and loving and friendly
I want Bobby on the inside, a tough core to protect me
I want them to start to love each other
So I can start to like me.

JENNY BLYTH

*Bobby was a nickname for me when I was a very tomboyish child.*


## Going home

There is a hole in my heart
which bleeds where childhood should be
and a prison in my head
where I keep that memory.

I come alive at midnight
when it's safe to be alone
and the darkness of my dreams
can be laid to rest till dawn.

My house, it has no callers
through the cold and dirty hall.
The warder hides in corners
and keeps my child in thrall.

No welcome here to friendship
while I'm caught in bounds of shame:
doing time within myself,
banged up by forgotten pain.

I sleepwalk through confusion
up to the parapet's edge
and looking over on my life
cry in wakening knowledge.

STEVE WILLIAMS

## Letter to Steven

You can come out now.

You can come out of the dark
and blood and ruins.
Out of the fearful shadowland.

Come and join me, my little friend.
I am not alive without you
and you are unhappy in that dark forgotten place,
hiding on the edge of mind,
from all those years ago.

I am afraid of what you know
but not afraid of you.
I want to hold you in my arms
and tell you it's all right,
you're safe now.

When you are ready you can speak to me,
and I will not be forced to betray you.

From Steven

STEVE WILLIAMS

In between, I imagined I was somebody else. You know how some kids have an imaginary friend? Well, I had one and I *hated* her. *She* did all the bad things, not me. I got on with being good and avoided her like the plague. She came into action when Grandad did. The rest of the time I ignored her. I guess it meant I didn't have to think about it, or *feel* anything. I could imagine I didn't even know. It took a lot of energy to stop her leaking through, especially at night, but I kept her up for years. Funny, even in my mid-twenties, when I first started to talk about what my Grandad did to me, it all seemed to come out in the "third person"—it was so automatic to think that way. My alienation from that part of me was very thorough—it had to be, to survive. But as an adult I found I just couldn't maintain the split—it no longer served me to project part of myself outside. It just got in the way. Whenever life got stressful, I found myself deluged with feelings I couldn't understand, and distant memories terrorized my sleep. It is scary, facing the truth and owning it, allowing yourself to *feel* and think about it all—but it's the only way to begin to break free. That's what I've found, though it was a hard choice to make.

It all "finished" when I was thirteen. I got pregnant in the Christmas holiday. By the time I missed my second cycle I was panic-stricken and very confused. I tried taking pills, but I couldn't go through with it. By the end of February I miscarried. I guess in many ways that was a relief—it solved a lot of decisions about what to do and who to tell—but it was hard to handle. I felt so guilty that this little child had lost her life. She seemed so incredibly innocent. It seemed so wrong that she should die and I should live. She had been so *alive* in my deadness.

Anyway, Grandad stopped after that. There just wasn't a "next time"—no great showdowns. It was getting risky. Circumstances changed and the opportunities just weren't there any more.

I still have no children, though I have been married for seven years and have been "trying" for more than four. How far this is to do with what he did—who knows? I did have an ectopic this year. Actually, although this was traumatic, I feel it was an important time of transition for me. I had a chance to grieve for that first child too. And

I was able to blow away some of the shadows and guilt that lurked around the whole thing of getting pregnant. I moved on.

JO ANNE

---

My next meeting with my counselor was a different ordeal altogether, we talked about "me as a five-year-old" and what I felt for that part of me . . . I found myself hating her for "not telling." I knew if I had told my parents right at the onset of the abuse, they would have stopped it then and there and I would not have experienced the sex and shame into my teenage years.

The knowledge was like a flashlight of knowing that all the self-loathing throughout my adult life had an origin. My counselor had helped me flick the switch. No amount of hearing "it's not your fault" helped me, I just knew I could have stopped it, but chose not to, so why . . .

Here my subconscious "kicked in" with an almost supernatural dream—I found myself hanging upside down on a trapeze with a shark below, coming out of the water trying to bite me.

In my adult form I was thinking: all I need to do is swing up and, it can't reach me. So I did and I was safe. Then I was sitting at the water's edge holding a babe in my arms. My counselor asked me about the child—but I said *she* had no face or age, I just knew she was very young.

I saw the shark coming but I thought I was out of reach, but he came right out of the water taking the child right out of my arms. Then I flashed to seeing the woman who was me—screaming silently—she was no longer me, I was watching. The next question was: "If you could be the woman again what would you say to the child in your arms, before and after the shark attack?"

I was caught off guard by the obscurity of the question.

I didn't know the shark would do what it did: the child could never have even seen it coming, she was safe in my arms, not under any threat, it happened so quickly. "The child could never have known," I kept repeating. "Well," said my counselor. "That's innocence," and I knew the truth of it.

All the anger hinged on me thinking as an adult—but all this happened to a five-year-old who could never have known danger lay with her brother then. All manner of things may have stopped her telling; after all, he never physically hurt her—he may have just said don't tell and she had listened, not wanting to get him into trouble . . .

SARA LOHMEYER

## Leave-ing

Nurtured gently in bud
Softly folded
Borne up above the mass,
The tender preludes to leaf-form
Rest and surge,
Bide and replicate,
Preparing for their emergence:
New leaves, kin of old.
A restatement of life's growth.

Each pristine year, as sun ripens,
Days lengthen,
A miracle of nature recreated
In the image of generations.
And yet each born anew
Bears its own subtle differences,
Mind over matter:
Intracellular variations
Yielding organic change.

It is the leaving,
That sad, departing season
Helios retiring,
Green life withering
Creating autumnal tints,

Which is life's inspiration.
For within ourselves do we not recreate
The bliss of re-enacted life force
As we watch life's vital decay?

Just as with Gaia's verdant foliage
Are we endowed with rebirth:
Chanced upon in season's heptate time
Glimpsed only by the scient ones
Primed for self-reaction,
Utilizing nature's blueprint and her force
Yet sensitive to infinite idiosyncrasies:
Patterning and repatterning,
A subtle transformation of will.

So I become my only pattern-maker
No past generational shade
May reimpose his will on mine,
Nor fetal-material yearning constrict
The form which my life takes:
I may be reborn
In my own image wholly
My soul inheritance affirmed.
Knowing in the past: being in the present.

CARO

*With love and thanks (—to my therapist)*

ANGIE MORTIMER-FARTHIN

# Learning to dance

Each of the contributions to this chapter, in its own way, addresses what can only be described as beginning to heal and the various ways in which this has been approached. This chapter differs from "Claiming the right to feel pain," in that the emphasis here has shifted from doing what we need to do in order to survive, to a point where we can recognize that we are beginning to heal. "Rite of passage" neatly illustrates this shift: the scars that remain after "cutting up" are regarded by the author as her battle honors.

Healing comes in numerous guises and we have tried to include as many in this chapter as possible. These range from being able to do things that we thought we'd never be able to do, through spirituality, nature and education, to the positive impact that good relationships with therapists and members of self-help groups can have. A few examples from this chapter illustrate something of this diversity. B.W.W.'s experiences of healing included being part of a survivors' group, reflexology, acupuncture, deep body massage and being a Shamanic dancer. In "Healing—an incredible experience" Angie gives an account of the highly successful relationship she has with her therapist, while Beth, in "Sisters in truth," explores the vital role that her self-help group continues to play in her healing.

## A true story about dreams

I am eight years old and I am standing in the school playing field. Other children look up at the sky with astonishment as a small aircraft circles lower and lower, until it is low enough to start unloading boxes which fall to the ground like Red Cross parcels. They are for me. I am not astonished because I have been waiting for them, but I had not really believed they would ever arrive. The other children watch in admiration as I start to open the boxes and reveal all the beautiful things that are just for me.

Shimmering beautiful dresses tumble out, covered with lace and jewels. Silk and velvet, singing pinks and kingfisher blues and golden yellows. And the jewels—bracelets, necklaces, tiaras; rubies, sapphires, emeralds, diamonds. Shawls and veils and shoes—oh, the shoes! Pink satin dancing shoes with pointed toes, embroidered with seed pearls—dozens and dozens of pairs. All this great richness and abundance for me, because at last I have been recognized and favored, at last I am comforted and honored. At last the hunger in my soul is filled.

This was my dream. I used it to comfort myself at night in bed when I was lonely and afraid, to help myself go to sleep. I never told anyone my fantasy because it would have shamed me to reveal my deprivation and my need; the deprivation which was seldom alleviated, the need that was so denied. I knew (but did not know) that I was different from other girls of my age, set apart and lonely. I felt it all through me but could not admit it to myself.

I had another dream too, which was also deeply comforting. In this one, I am playing with my best friend Sophy and we are climbing on the greenhouse. I accidentally slip and fall through the glass. I am cut all over and bleeding dangerously. Sophy, horrified, runs as fast as she can to get help; Sophy's father comes, and he carries me to the house and calls an ambulance. Sophy's mother bandages me. I have a broken leg too. Soon I am in hospital with my leg in plaster, and people around my bed, all worried about me and showing warm concern and anxiety for me. I do not imagine feeling any pain, but only a great relief that my wounds can be seen and attended to. I bask in the loving attention that I receive.

I *was* wounded, but the bleeding was inside. The crippling was inside. No one saw and no one comforted me.

I grew to be an adult and tried to live as though nothing was wrong inside me. But I was still crippled and still bleeding, and after a few years the anesthetic of denial and amnesia began to wear off and I started to feel the pain of my wounds. Often it seemed intolerable. There were many times when I wished I was dead, just so that the pain would stop. I developed a new fantasy—different ways to commit suicide. The image I found most arresting was of myself lying dead in a bath filled with warm water, dressed in a long white gown, with swirls of blood curling around me from my opened veins. The classical Roman style. One night I dreamt that I saw a young dead girl in a bath filled with blood; in the same dream were babies impaled on long kitchen knives. Many of my sleeping dreams were filled with intruders, molesters, pursuers and other more graphic horrors.

Despite this, letting the pain through was the start of healing. It is nine years since I began to acknowledge my pain, to remember and recognize what had been done to me as a child, and to begin my recovery. Now I can talk about it and try to tell people how much it hurt, and still hurts. Often they do not want to hear. I am still lonely, and still hungry in my soul.

I am learning to dance. I started attending class once a week and gradually began to improve. My movements have become more and more fluid and graceful, my body more flexible and free. My confidence has grown; other people praise me. Sometimes I even feel beautiful. A woman in the class told me that my arm movements were so lovely that when she practiced at home she tried to visualize my arms and copy the way I used them in dancing. One evening, the teacher asked the class to improvise to a piece of music which was slow and haunting and melodic; although Arabic, it had a Slavonic quality. The class danced, and when the music was over the teacher said, "I'm going to play it again, and I want you all to watch while Emily dances. This is Emily's music!"

I danced again. I felt the music as though it was coming from my body, and I danced my loneliness and my longing. When the music finished, I was astonished to see that my teacher had tears on her face. She came over to me and said "That was beautiful!" and then she hugged me.

A part of my mind still refuses to believe that this really happened. It must have been a mistake, it was meant for someone else, it was a fluke and I will never be able to dance in the same way again . . . but nevertheless, I have been asked to dance to that music at the Concert. A part of me fears that I will stumble or fall or be graceless, but another part of me fears what might happen if I dance too well—who might be watching who will punish me if I reach too openly for beauty, for joy and for life?

But I am going to perform, and I am making a beautiful costume of shining gold and shimmering rainbow colors, covered in sequins and beads that sparkle like jewels.

When June comes, a lonely woman with lovely arms will step into the spotlight and dance.

EMILY BIRD

EMILY BIRD AND A SMALL FRIEND

## Meditation circle dance

Fluidity and grace . . . fluidity and grace
Echoing in my mind.
Unity . . . pain . . . separateness.
What gets in the way
keeping me from connecting
self to self . . . to others . . . to higher power.

Then . . . as one lung
The nine of us
Moving in, moving out
Breathing in, breathing out
Separate, but together.
The smooth ease of letting go . . .
. . . and flowing . . .
My breath "taken from me" . . .
The wonder of it.
Candles flickering in the dark
Eyes lidded.

An overwhelming warmth
of love enveloping me,
Seeming to flow around the circle
Being received and returned,
received and returned
Slowly awakening in me
A soft gentle quietness . . .
Gentle . . . gentle . . . gentle . . .

NARELLE DOUGLAS

# Serendipity

Serendipity
Pleasing discovery of the unexpected
My body suddenly significant
No appeals
No amnesty
Movies in the mind
Played out to solitary intercourse
Longing for your company
For sex . . .
For love . . .
For me . . .
For you . . .
My Grand Piano
Oh please . . .
Please play it again!

JAN CHAPPLE (NÉE DURKIN)

---

I feel it's terribly important to get the right therapy or it can do more damage than good. Any therapy that doesn't empower you, enabling you to stand on your own two feet, is useless. I feel now the only good therapy occurs in survivors' groups; where there is a balance of power and every person is an "expert." The only other therapists I trust are my acupuncturist and a woman who gives me reflexology, deep body massage with aromatherapy oils and reiki healing. These two people have also taught me how to keep myself healthy and in balance.

The most empowering experiences I have had has been through North American Indian medicine wheel teachings and ceremonies. I am now a Shamanic dancer and although I still experience fear I can now embrace it; dance through it and move with the rhythm of my own heartbeat, deeply connected to Grandmother Earth's heartbeat.

One of the most important factors of healing is to create a safe space and to trust ourselves. After all we are the only ones who truly know what we went through and how *we* felt. It stands to reason therefore that *we* are the only ones who know how to heal ourselves.

B.W.W.

## Sisters in truth

This room is full of courage.
I look around and I see faces,
Faces full of pain and hurt,
Women whose lives echo my own.
Each time I enter this room
I am filled with love,
And hope for the future.
Their courage shines from them,
Like a beacon in the dark night.
They comfort me when I am sad,
They encourage me when I falter.
They support me on my lonely journey,
My journey to the past,
Into my nightmares.
They are there with me always,
Laughing and loving and giving.
I shall hold them in my heart for ever.
They make me feel wanted and cared for,
They have led me back to sanity.
For when I am with them,
I know I am real, alive, and truthful.
I no longer roam in darkness and uncertainty,
Their truths fill my mind and bring me peace.
I shall love them always,
They are my true family,
My sisters in truth.

BETH (2)

## Get the Jew

Shattering,
Fucking shit,
Arsehole—
Revenge!
Ramming,
Rigid,
Coming.

Hands—
Grabbing at him,
Pawing,
At me.

Hold him down,
Hold him down.
Get the Jew,
Get the Jew,
Get the Jew.
Sinister,
Watching them
Getting the Jew—
Me—

RON WIENER

### The therapeutic recall

*Brian:* "I want to share with you what happened when I was five. I was sent away to a holiday camp. I was the only Jewish boy there. One night we were left on our own except for one counselor, that's what I think they were called. The rest were off at a party or something. The other boys caught me in a dorm and they put me on a blanket and threw me up into the air, higher and higher and I called out and no one came and then they held me down, these older boys, twelve or thirteen years old and they tore my pajamas off and someone grabbed at my willy and someone spat on me and then they forced me on to my knees and one of them jerked my head back and another forced his dick into my mouth and he came and his stuff dribbled out and from the corner of my eye I saw the counselor standing there, watching, and then there was another boy in my mouth and then I was thrust down on a bed, face down and I was gagging from the sperm and then someone was on top of me and they were shouting to get the Jew and they forced themselves into me, time and time again. I called out; no one came, and again and again, and then they were gone and I was left alone except for the counselor standing there in the dark at the edge of the room and he picked up a blanket and he put it over me and then he turned and left and I was alone and I've been alone ever since."

The group sat in stunned silence. Slowly one of the women moved and held Brian and started to rock him and the rest sat, holding hands and watching over them as the sun set in the corner of the room.

RON WIENER

## Peeling back the layers

With the short black knife
I cut and score the skin
As if describing lines of longitude
About a living globe
And, maintaining a delicate balance
Between gentleness and strength,
I remove the pellucid outer rind
To expose the orange flesh,
Fragrant in its segmental translucence.

Or, I seize the blade
And with slashes to tip and base
Tear away the integument
Of shrivelled, desiccated skin

Then grasping the inner fleshy bulb
I cut clear through
Releasing a pungent, milky exudate
Which irritates my delicate humors.
Yields scalding, blinding tears.

Or, within this women's room
I flex my invisible blade
Wanting so much to trust,
To pare myself in my honesty
To peel back the outmoded pellicle
To free my innermost life processes
From their eternal darkroom
And shed light upon my soul.
That I may connect.

But the knives of fear flash.
Their cutting edges honed
By eons of grinding isolation
Forcing me, on pain of life,
To reveal my utter nakedness
To expose myself to mortification,
Raucous laughter, searing jibes.
In terror I tighten the shroud.
What am I doing here?

And yet I will return in hope
And perhaps, with time,
I shall give credence to their wise words
Recognize the familiar patterns of anguish,
Acknowledge our mutual fates
In screams of whispered desolation,
Begin to share my pain
Through excoriating teardrops
Transforming into crystals of amber.

CARO

I look back over all these years [of therapy] and see how much and how often I was disempowered and abused in various ways; how ethical issues sometimes became the tool for some kinds of abuse, how my trust was betrayed, how my being a victim was taken advantage of, how my therapy sometimes became therapy to heal the abuse of therapy, how concepts such as transference and projection were sometimes used to deny my reality: for example my seeing real damage happening in the present was said to be simply my transference feelings. So often, theories and concepts were used to enable the therapist to control me and as a wall to protect himself. I think, too, of how my paid-for time was often taken up by counter-transference issues that were not recognized. I think one of the most disempowering and constantly repeated abuses was the denial of my feelings, my truth, my process. Fragile and fractured though it was, it was always there trying to be heard.

When I look back and ask myself in what way and how much has therapy empowered me, I can say only inasmuch as I was re-spected and believed and listened to, only inasmuch as my process was accepted and worked with, only inasmuch as my reality was val-idated, only inasmuch as the exploration was a shared experience and not under someone else's control, only inasmuch as there was safety, only inasmuch as there was a certain degree of flexibility and will-ingness to hear my story, only inasmuch as there was openness and honesty and genuineness and a meeting.

And the worst part of it all has been my vulnerability as a client, my having no one to turn to or support me, my having to try to do battle with or make things safe for therapists while totally alone, and my having to do that from the weaker position of client while in the midst of the distress caused by the various sorts of hurt and/or abuse, in order to try to protect myself. It has been horrific that the severe abuse that happened to me originally has been the cause of more abuse. It was terrible not to be heard, not to be believed. It was terrible to be encouraged to trust and then to have that trust be-trayed, to trust and not be trusted. It was horrific to have my barriers broken down and then be hurt in ways that were beyond my capacity to take or protect myself from; being unable to protect myself or leave because my need to heal was so great.

And in the same way as I have been helped in therapy by those helping me believing and witnessing and supporting me, I have been helped by those who were able to believe and witness and support me when the therapeutic situation became damaging, especially if the therapist himself was able to take that on and admit the mistake and help me to work through the hurt.

BRENDA NICKLINSON

## Hello little girl

Hello little girl.
You are beautiful and soft.
I love the unruly curl of your hair,
Your trusting, brown eyes,
Your smiling mouth,
Your rounded limbs and body,
The way you stroke your chilly earlobes,
Your unspoken need for love.

You did not deserve the plunder,
The violation of your soul
To which your child-life laid you bare,
For if the elders in your life
Did not act as your protectors,
How could you walk the treacherous slope
From infancy to womanhood
And survive unharmed?

I weep for your lost innocence,
I flinch at the anguish of your youth.
Your body remembers and suffers for you
In the aftermath of forced intimacy,

Which has left you abandoned, isolated,
Unable to make one spontaneous reaction:
Bound by the reflex of familiarity
To those times endured and long forgotten.

But little girl you still remain
Within that fragile, adult body
And you are still beautiful and soft,
Still gentle, generous, engaging.
You retain your vulnerability,
Your inability to trust yourself and others
But you continue to shine.
Your light will never be extinguished.

Come little girl, take my hand
We shall hold each other firmly,
Reflecting each in the other's eyes
For we are not two but one:
I, the fearful, distorted woman
You, the simple, playful girl-child.
Together we will rediscover
True integrity in truth revealed.

CARO

---

I have been trying to write a short account of my journey over the last three years. That was when, at the age of fifty, I started to recover repressed memories of sexual abuse in my family, which until then I had thought was a perfectly normal, well-functioning one. With the help of my excellent counselor I have gradually become aware through dream writing, dream work, body memories and specific gestalt work, that I was used by both my parents, separately and together as a sexual object being frequently and grossly sexually assaulted. At the same time I was involved in a satanic cult whenever we stayed with my maternal grandparents—several times a year. I realized I used disassociation to cope with all the abuse and then managed to cut the whole thing out of my conscious memory after it stopped when I was about five.

I was amazed to think that I had escaped relatively unscathed from this incredibly abusive childhood, the only abnormal behavior being that of crying very easily and frequently. This did not stop me becoming a nurse, a midwife, a health visitor and finally a Relate counselor. I am also a wife and mother of three adult children, all of whom are reasonably well-adjusted human beings.

JULIA

## Healing—an incredible experience

The therapist I am working with trained as a humanistic psychotherapist. She firmly believes that the client, not the therapist, knows the best way to heal. She is also prepared to be flexible about how long sessions last and how frequently they occur. This has allowed me the freedom I needed to work at my own pace and in my own way. For many months it seemed that my main therapy process took place between sessions and that I used my therapist more as a receiver of what I brought and a witness to my process. Certainly, for a long time, I was telling her *about* what was going on and not directly experiencing anything while I was with her. During these sessions I would often experience intense body writhings which could be very painful but resulted in an undoing of the physical tension that bound my body. All my life my whole body had felt painful and heavy and I had assumed that everyone lived like that. Now that I am free of the physical discomfort, that I no longer have hunched shoulders nor wear a collar, I realize what a sorry state I was in physically. I have used painting, drawing, left-hand/right-hand dialoguing, inner child work, visualization, meditation, working with clay, movement and anything at all that might help. I have also made use of various weekend workshops, aerobics, Tai Chi and the Alexander technique to assist in my healing. It's been hard work. Now I know what is meant by living; before, I merely existed as best I could.

I got married when I was twenty-two. Here I was with a husband who loved me and whom I wanted to love but I knew that if I let myself get close to him he would suffer. I just couldn't understand myself at all. I couldn't explain what was going on yet I felt he was so stupid not to realize the danger he was in. And always there was this cry deep inside me: "This isn't the way it should be—what's wrong with me?"

When I was twenty-three I gave birth to my first child and that was the beginning of my journey towards healing although it wasn't until twenty-four years later that I began to recover memories of sexual abuse and my life started to make sense. My baby was two weeks overdue and I had an induced labor. I remember the consultant saying, "This baby just doesn't want to be born." That wasn't the problem. *I* didn't want this baby to be born. I wanted this baby so much yet the only way it could be born was to pass through me and in doing it would become contaminated—and I could do nothing to stop that happening.

I had two more children, suffered an eleven-year depression, and fought tooth and nail every day to keep a hold on my sanity. I did a good job too. On the outside I think I appeared relatively "normal"—I was certainly terrified that if anyone ever discovered what was going on inside me my children would be taken from me and I would be locked up. I also suffered a complete memory blackout which lasted about six hours. This was a terrifying experience and, once again, I didn't dare tell anyone what had happened. Very slowly over the following years my memory began to fill in and continues to do so. I feel now that both the depression and memory blank were defenses to shut out memories I couldn't face at the time.

When I was forty-six I went to a therapist for what I thought was to be a few sessions. Little did I know what was to come. I found myself having the oddest experiences. Strange dreams (I had never dreamt before). Transfixions—when I would suddenly find myself standing stock still staring ahead of me and quite unable to move. Hearing a screaming child deep inside me and not being able to help her in any way. Having very strong physical sensations of hands on me. Having flashes when I would see parts of a man's body. Inexplicable feelings of terror. And on and on. So many sensations, so strong and yet seemingly attached to nothing. My thinking mind could make no sense of all this and recoiled from what my body was telling me. I believe I was sexually abused between three and ten years of age.

I went through the most amazing birth experiences. Both of being born and of me giving birth. From where I am now I think I was literally giving birth to my "self," the "self" that had been so damaged the first time.

I also had a long period where I carried within me my "split." Three little children . . . these three children became a reality for me for many months and I worked with them in many ways. I used left-hand writing and dialogued with them, I took them on shopping trips and bought what they wanted, I took them on walks and bicycle rides. I tuned in to them and slowly learned which parts of me they were depicting. Eventually I bought three wee rag dolls and carried them with me . . . After a time the angry child grew up, then the hurt child grew up and by doing so they seemed to merge with the little girl who then became my own deeply hurt inner child. It wasn't until this integration happened that I could begin working with my childhood pain which, until this took place, went virtually unacknowledged by me.

I made two life-sized dolls. First a baby doll which I spent hours holding and cuddling and nurturing. I was giving myself what I had so missed—mothering. Then I made a child doll of about three years old and spent time with her, listening to her story, giving her attention, giving her what I had needed at the time I was first abused and there was no one there to help me. All this was immensely healing and I gradually became less and less self-conscious about what was going on and less and less worried that I was going mad or that someone would discover what I was doing and lock me up. Although I couldn't really understand what was happening to me I went with it and I became more and more sure of my own sanity and my own healing. For the first time in my life I became unafraid of being me.

I experienced many different forms of dreams, which would occur night or day. Some were like still-life shots, some were like a video turning on in my head and a "film" would be running. And one incredible night I seemed to be inside my mind, as though in a factory, and having a tour round all the parts that were responsible for different functions.

Poetry began to surface. Quite suddenly I would find a poem was there and I had to write it down. So many of them and so evocative.

The fact that I still have no cognitive memory of being abused does bother me. My family greeted my disclosure with denial and consternation. I had hoped, perhaps naively, for confirmation. I feel I can't verify what was, and still is, coming up and can, occasionally, be flooded with doubts—have I made all this up? However I cannot argue with my improving mental health and general feeling.

I am astonished at what I have achieved over the last two and a half years while all this was going on. I gave up my job, which had become my life. I did a foundation course with the Open University, a certificate course on counselling, trained as a bereavement counselor and am now doing a part-time diploma in client-centered counselling.

Our marriage, after twenty-seven long, hard years, is finally coming together. Now it's as though we have reached the point where other people start. I can be myself. I am also immensely grateful that I have got free of the prison I was in, that my husband and I are still together and that we have a second chance. We are making the most of it and we are succeeding.

ANGIE

---

I have discovered that depression is just a mask that anger
    wears when fear holds my reins,
a quilt to smother rage.
If I can but lift the corner, fury pours like meltdown through
    my blood,
my rage rears up, bronze cast, a warrior.
I seize a sword and slay the dragon,
gird my loins and find the minotaur,
storm the palisades, kill the enemy,
avenge the children, staunch their blood, heal their wounds;
go to Jocasta's hell, where incest burns,
and annihilate those with God's millstone round their necks;
the abusers of children,
the double demand,
I would take their lives as they took ours.

LIZZY COTTRELL

## Becoming whole again

Through therapy I learned about myself. I have been able to allow myself to experience feelings. I have learned that trust is not an all or nothing thing. In December last year my multiple selves came together during a therapy session. My therapist asked me if I could visualize myself as both child and adult in the room. When I had, he asked what the child needed from the adult to make her feel safe. I described what I saw happening: the child and adult held hands, stood up to walk towards me and then stopped. My therapist asked if I could get them to come closer together. As they drew closer I saw another form, to one side, not clear, and told the therapist. He said to ignore it and concentrate on getting the adult and child closer. Suddenly all three merged and rushed forward. I felt them come into me and cried and laughed. When I could speak again I tried to describe what had happened. I could only say it felt like a star burst. It was the most painful and yet wonderful feeling I could imagine.

CHRIS

## The wall

A strong, hard wall,
Forms a block,
A solid boundary,
No way through.
But one by one,
The bricks come down
A smile, a nod,
A hug and cuddle
The barrier breaks
Bit by bit,
But invisible to all
Including this girl

A kiss, a touch,
The cracks begin,
And still the girl
Sees solid wall
But very soon
Deftly done
The barriers down
The boundary smashed.

SARAH


## Tears

The tears you cry are tears of hope
that wash away your sorrow
ready to fight another day
for there always is a tomorrow

CILLA


## Healing

Did I frighten you, or can't you stand the sight of tears?
I have to try to breathe again inside,
to let my pain flow out.
When I nurse it, hold it, feed it
then I burn inside.

I must hold myself in the palm of my own hand,
comfort and protect myself,
nurture the little flicker of wholeness—

JULIE COCKBURN

## My secret baptism

Standing in rain
soaking my clothes
cleansing my flesh
so nobody knows.
Why I'm standing in rain
soaking my skin
baptizing my secret
I'm cleansing my sins.
Cleansing my body
healing my soul
taking back purity
regaining control.

SELINA NICHOLAS

---

Recently I confided in someone that I've known for a few years. Though we are not the best of friends, it was essential that I told someone.

I could no longer contain the mass of confusion that increased rapidly over the months. I was particularly ill at the time, experiencing terrible panic attacks and other physical ailments.

I now know that this was part of the healing process. I felt relieved that a weight had been lifted off me. I do feel guilty about telling her my intimate secret. I wonder how she is coping with such a burden and how she relates to me now. I wouldn't want her to feel that I'm dependent on her.

JOAN FROM CHESHIRE

CLARE MITCHELL

*(This photo is part of a record of a piece of live art entitled "Coming clean.")*

It's been really difficult living in a body which grows to look like him. I've had real problems trying to be male anyway. It's taken a long while to pull him out of my head. One thing I've done is to write a lot of stuff down day by day just to stop it whizzing around in my head. Find that I can talk about it with Nancy. Therapy can be contradictory. I want to be in control of my life and yet it can feel like I'm constantly reporting back each week or because of transference and using Nancy as a focus for my difficult feelings.

It's been a complex thing to sort out but I am really impressed now that I did everything I could not be like him. One escape was into my intellect but it was hard to reveal this. I still find I can't express myself in words or speech as well as I'm thinking. It's a bit scary opening up my refuge like that. It's also frustrating as I want to exist outside this part of my personality and currently I feel very confused about what I want to do. I'm in the middle of a part time MA in Philosophy of Mind, although I'm taking a year out at the moment because last year got to be a real mess as I was beginning to break through all my protective layers into the suppressed emotion. It made me a very scary person to be around.

One thing I did for this was that for a couple of weeks I virtually locked myself away and became very spiritual. Everything spoke to me, had significance and I wrote about 200 pages trying to separate and explain my life as being separate from him. Going into all the anger, rage and sorrow, using a division of natural for me and unnatural for him. It involved a lot of ritual I invented for myself (or maybe I was guided by some Divine power—I think so, anyway—I call her Mother Peace). Lots of red wine, white candles and cleansing baths to wash the dirt away. I also have a tree in a local park which is my connection with her and I commune with it for brief periods. It helped me start to feel connected with the world as my previous vision of myself was isolated, with the rest of everything behind a glass wall.

KEVIN WENDAR

SANDRA BARNES

## Being a "survivor," what did I learn in order to survive?

To put other people's needs first
To make myself invisible
To blot out intolerable realities
To efface myself
To merge with the identities of others
To become the occluded soul
To leave my body
To internalize my anger, transforming it into fear and guilt
To cut off from my fear, sadness and self-love
To doubt myself
To doubt myself in relation to others
To avoid intimacy
To disconnect from and distrust my sexuality and sexual
        boundaries
To put myself down, to denigrate my life and my
        achievements

To act out of self-hatred and a desire to destroy myself
To live in chaos, seeking perfect control, too afraid to act,
    fearing I would experience total powerlessness
To see life as a series of crises to be got through, to see
    pleasure as guilt ridden, unreal or untrustworthy

What am I learning now to live my potential?

To put my needs first
To be aware of myself
To be present with my whole reality
To assert myself
To experience my boundaries
To connect with and earth my spiritual self
To stay in my body
To feel and externalize my anger
To feel and express my fear, sadness and self-love
To trust myself
To trust myself in relation to others
To risk intimacy
To know and trust my sexuality and sexual boundaries
To celebrate myself, my life, my achievements
To act out of self-love and a desire for fulfillment
To live in order and chaos, seeking a balance, trusting in my
    own power and open to the flow of life
To see life as an evolutionary challenge, to celebrate each day
    with love, rest, fun and spiritual connection

ABIGAIL ROBINSON

## The invisible elephant

Acknowledging my childhood sexual abuse has caused me to redefine
my notion of what a strong person is, along with many other archaic
notions which are no longer appropriate.

Strong people survive the things that hurt them. To some extent they may avoid hurt, but they can't avoid everything. It's how you deal with the hurt that makes you a strong person. It takes courage to deal with it, rather than tucking it away in a corner to fester and make you feel weak and worthless. Courage is being scared, but recognizing that and doing "it" anyway.

As far as dealing with all the issues and hurts of childhood sexual abuse is concerned, I have found it's like an elephant—huge and unavoidable once revealed. The only way to eat an elephant is one bit at a time, the joke tells us. Fortunately, each bite gives you the energy and strength to deal with the next.

I'm eating my elephant one bite at a time, knowing that I can't eat it all in one go, knowing that I can't avoid any of the bites (hurts) or I won't have the strength for the next, but also knowing that eventually I will eat it all. Having done that, I know I will be a stronger person.

It's this aspect of myself which I admire—I have done, and do, what I have to do to survive. Moreover, I set myself targets and I achieve them. I am proud of how far I have come. I am successful on my own terms. I am an achiever and I give *myself* credit for the positive things that come from dealing with my childhood sexual abuse. The world gives me credit for the things *it* values, like academic success, being a member of a professional body, or finding a job with promotion or better pay. I give myself the credit for those things too. Being able to give myself a pat on the back was one bite of my elephant, and enjoying it another! Nothing gives me as much reward, though, as eating my own invisible elephant.

I feel very lucky to have been able to contribute to this anthology. In a way it is a celebration of survivors eating their own elephants and making them visible in the process. Survivors deserve admiration for whichever way they choose to eat their own elephants.

ANONYMOUS

## Rite of passage

These scars that I wear like ornaments,
that I refuse to cover in order to spare you,
they are a badge, a symbol of new dignity.
If they offend you, turn away, talk to
someone else, do not apologize for your
revulsion. Sometimes they do that to me.
But still I will not cover them.
The marks are a reminder of past horrors.
Still livid in my mind—though faded
on my skin—as a pale blue tattoo
on the wrist of an old man who still
smells the ovens of Nelsen.
I passed my tests of courage beyond
the call of duty, emerged from the battle
both weary and scarred
But I AM HERE.
I AM ALIVE.
I survived my rites of passage and
decorated my skin with my own
battle honors.
And no, I will not cover them to
spare you.
These scars are both my shame
and my pride.
Despite them—or maybe because I am whole at last.

CAROLE BISHOP

## Walking out of hell

The discovery of my abuse happened at the age of eighteen. Until that point in my life the scars of behavior built into my character had spiralled me into a dark underworld. I was heavily centered within drugs, prostitution and crime. Fortunately I had not experienced prostitution, although I was easy prey for anyone. I had allowed various partners to use me. It was my way to obtain love, by allowing people to walk through me!

My mind was the first to go. A huge paranoia built around me. I trusted nobody and believed everyone wanted to kill me and hurt me psychologically, emotionally, physically and spiritually. I quit the drugs and took refuge in my mother's home. I had now walked straight into agoraphobia, which lasted for a year. I saw nobody, I feared the outside and felt evil and panicky around people. I felt trapped as if surrounded by glass, I could not tell my pain: it continued to twist me inside and keep my soul on fire. I saw nobody except a gentle aunt who was very neutral and open-minded.

My emotions followed and began to erupt intensely after numerous panic attacks. A panic attack felt like a heart attack. When having one I disappeared and shrank so far, I was a dot inside of myself and could only see the shell of my body shaking uncontrollably. Outside everyone seemed so far away. I broke! I felt and believed that I was in hell!! I wanted to die and yet something inside just hung on desperately. How I survived is a mystery: all was grey and my insides lead and yet hope glinted from within at me. I sobbed, wrenching from the heart in confusion. My doctor put me on to a counselor. I tested out trust with her and she gave me floods of hope. At this point she was my lifeline. I lived for the hour a week when I saw her; she was a new door to peace.

A detective began to emerge within me and my counselor—Maria—helped guide me into my erased life. I discovered that my mother had left when I was seven years old. How could I forget? As the pain breathed I saw myself being raped by my father through a long-forgotten memory. This memory stained for six months, it hung like a picture in my mind between me and the present. Every man, every color my father wore, his mannerisms in people on TV or in other men, every tiny impulse of his reminded me of the abuse and sent me into fear. I became obsessed about the abuse day and night. My nightmares merged into my reality. I could never tell them apart. I found an incest survivors' group in the local telephone directory. I joined and it was like a golden magic circle built on others' love and support.

Life was so unbearable living with my mother and stepfather. I kept having flashes and seeing them as Myra Hindley and Ian Brady. This made me label myself as insane and dangerous. I told myself that I was a dirty pervert. They always seemed so huge, distant and intimidating. I had a great suspicion of them, yet I continued to doubt myself, which drove me crazy. One of the women at the incest support group worked at a youth hostel and organized a room for me. I was so scared of my mother and stepfather yet I craved my mother's love. *But why?* Why was I afraid!

Years on and I remembered my mother sneaking into my room when I was four years old and raping me. Around six months on and I became obsessed with my mother's cleaning habits. I felt sick whenever she cleaned. Bleach gave me nausea, and when anybody else cleaned I felt scared and small. I felt I was going crazy again. Then at a counselling session I took my mother's tea towel with me. I prattled on about this and that, and then my hand grabbed the tea towel and I said "I have brought this. It's something to do with my mum's cleaning." WHOOSH! I was sobbing like a baby, wailing and shaking. I felt I had no skin and I could see my mother scrubbing me violently with bleach in boiling hot water. Every time I cried she shook me around the bath. I had to concentrate on being silent. Blood was everywhere: she scrubbed in between my legs, right inside my vagina. The blood was on my body, not coming from inside.

The image of my mother was crumbling. I believed she was an angel. Now she was beginning to look like a witch.

There was more inside; I could sense it. I had an unhealthy interest in witchcraft and black magic. Any mystical information kept me alive. I was scared of myself, needing to understand about black powers. I thought I was evil and deranged. Then a memory came to my aid in the form of a dream I had as a child.

I was six years old and running down the stairs. My dad had woken me and scared me into the sitting room. I could vaguely sense people sitting on the sofa. I tucked it away in my mind as a dream. The feelings though were so fearful. I could see a werewolf running down the stairs. Nobody would take my hand and help me on to the sofa. They sat, watched me squirm and laughed. The wolf drooled and breathed viciously. The television flickered. I saw Paul—my brother—sat on the sofa when I was eight. A cult film filled my mind with symbols, blood, rituals, and a wolf beast that was mating with a woman stained my mind. Even then as a child I felt questioning about the magic.

Two years with this new information and the fog gradually cleared on the memory. My mother, father, my now stepfather and his ex-wife awaited my arrival in the sitting room when I was six. They all had sex with me. At one point as Dad and Les—my stepfather—raped me my mother watched as I pleaded to her with my eyes to help. She told me to stay, and because I was her puppet I obeyed. They used pig's blood to smear on me and then threatened me with the pig's head in the oven. After this ritual my mother took me to the bathroom to scrub her guilt from me.

I have recently discovered the deep basement part of my emotions and found a new memory. I relived it, feeling small, physically shaking with fear and sobbing. Mum and Dad took me to a church place. People, lots of them, waited in cloaks, black ones. They sat me in a symbolic shape surrounded by candles. I was told to drink blood. They cut me and chanted. I was raped and offered to the devil. At the age of twenty-one I am still afraid that people I know are part of this organization. I live in a small town, the same one as when I was a child. I was threatened with death and brainwashed to keep me silent. I was told that the devil watched my every thought. I have always sieved my thoughts and swallowed any negative ones out of fear that God will condemn me for them. I felt watched, afraid to be me, to come out and be heard in case I was killed. All I have is anger. I have confronted my mother only to be disbelieved. My father has threatened me plenty, saying ugly trolls lived in the walls of our house and would watch me. I used to find relaxing very difficult: even on my own I sense eyes around me. My father is a neo-Nazi; he believes he is right. The torture: tying me up as a child, making me dress up for sex, pissing on me; holding a knife to my throat while raping and slightly slicing me; making me have sex with my friends, forcing my brother to rape me and my only trusted friend Arkley, our dog. He believes this is correct. He is into bad black powers and worships the devil.

I have found my life so hard to accept. One day all is normal and the next it caves in and I fall into hell.

I have healed so much and now I am in control of my mind and decisions. I am at present at college taking a two-year performing arts course. From being agoraphobic, I have faced my fears and now—can you imagine!—I am in plays, singing and dancing for people. In front of people and that's *courage!* Considering I could not be near people before! I have friends and workmates who love and trust me and speak highly of me and they are genuinely non-judgmental. I still have difficulty trusting this, but I can hear the compliments now and take them closer to my heart.

I'm not bad. The acts upon me were bad. I used my intelligence and child logic that pierced and shone through from the brainwashing labyrinth that my perpetrators built.

I AM ALIVE HERE AND NOW!

After pain comes joy

After the rain comes the sun

It's nature that nothing lasts for ever.

ANONYMOUS

## My plastic raincoat

It's taken me a long time but now I'm taking off my plastic raincoat, allowing myself to be exposed to all weathers. I've worn it virtually all my life, protecting myself against those bits in life that, although real, I preferred to pretend weren't there. I was quite a young child when I first tried it on and then throughout my life I've never properly taken it off. It grew with me and was part of me, with its pockets totally mis-shapen and bulging with excuses—mine. When I met anything I didn't like or couldn't cope with, on went my plastic "let's pretend" coat.

For every single one of us life is *not* a bowl of cherries. We all meet hurts, experiencing grief and pain when they hit us and knock us over. But wounds *do* heal, both the visible and invisible ones. But first we need to see and feel them, and allow the right ointment to be administered.

Wearing my raincoat this was impossible, as nothing could penetrate the plastic either way—neither inwards nor outwards—and I'd tightened the belt to the very last notch so that I could scarcely breathe. It all seemed so much easier than facing my life as it is and working through the old hurts—and growing!

But where did it get me? Exactly nowhere. One day I met a situation which confronted me with the old hurts, fear and guilt I had always managed to keep suppressed and half-strangled inside my raincoat. And there was an explosion—a volcanic eruption—and everything began to spill over and I couldn't stop it. I was powerless as it gushed down, threatening to swamp me. But, as before, along came the right person at the right time.

I was no longer a child playing "let's pretend." It was time to stop playing games and time to look, think and feel and sort out the good from the bad—throw away the useless rubbish. And after a while I realized that, as painful as it was, I was growing forwards, no longer stunted by past ghosts. You see, my friend took my hand and together we picked up the light that is God and hung on to it as we cleaned the cobwebs from the darkest corners and saw just what was there. I couldn't have done that wearing my plastic raincoat.

Everything just runs off plastic. It is non-absorbent and cold and becomes rigid in time. But once the air is allowed in, and then everything else, it's possible to look back at what we have known along the way over the years and appreciate just how valuable and relevant these experiences are right now—how they can be picked up and used in a very positive way.

Life is harder in the raw without the old protection. But it's *real*. The old crutches of "let's pretend" and "putting on a face" are crumbling as I meet myself just as I am and not as I think people would prefer to see me. It takes a lot of prayer and courage to take some things out of hiding and share them with another who needs them. But it's that person at that time who matters and who we can

perhaps help. Who cares what anybody else may think? It's off with
the plastic raincoat, leaving naked vulnerability exposed in the act
of recognizing and meeting the needs of another; of holding out love
and care and hoping that it will be used.

Six little words walk with me that say it all:
"Let go . . . Let be . . . Let God . . ." Through him everything is
possible. He'll keep me warm no matter how hard it rains now that
I've taken off my raincoat. He'll be glad to because I'm meeting myself so much more freely and honestly.

ANONYMOUS


## oh darling i have loved you

oh darling i have loved you
beyond the reach of time
and framed the memory of you
unconsciously in rhyme

i heard your cries of terror
and felt your deep despair
and struggled with the terror
of knowing you weren't there

yet you were never silent
and called without a sound
relentlessly insistent
you needed to be found

my own realization
which now i understand
is that our joint salvation
was synchronously planned

and all these years my torture
has been your very own
and i have been your future
and never even known

let's gather up the fragments
and make of them a feast
of selves in blended raiment
a miracle at least

BRENDA NICKLINSON

JANINE GUICE

Sources of help are a very individual choice. I have had both good and not so good and one positively bad experience. The responsibility upon those we may use is great and their expertise should be such that it can meet the very individual needs of their clients.

I turned initially to my GP, who referred me to a local mental health department. I became part of a group which aimed to support and provide therapy for people with a wide variety of needs. The group offered some positive aspects but was soon wound up for reasons only known to the department. I felt it did not meet the complex needs I had because it was not based on the specific area of childhood sexual abuse.

I returned to my GP and he referred me to a psychologist. Due to her poor health, sessions became erratic. I was offered someone else eventually but the offer was made in a rather uncaring way. I declined.

I moved jobs and requested, via my new GP, continuing help. I was referred to a psychiatrist. This was a dreadful experience. Having been subjected to strong drug therapy by my previous GP, I was unhappy when after a very brief first session I was given more drugs. The few sessions I had were all very brief, after enduring very long waits in a full waiting room. The expectation that I would go in and tell them what was wrong was almost farcical. I was told on one occasion by the stand-in psychiatrist that he couldn't help if I wasn't willing to tell him what was wrong. I had in total about ten minutes with this complete stranger who I guess was under pressure to get through the packed waiting room. As far as I was concerned this service was a grossly inadequate provision and a very poor use of NHS money. I never went back.

Next my GP referred me to the local psychologist. This again had limited benefit. Often appointments were changed, or there were very long waits, after which I was told that the session had to be canceled. The area where one waited was so open, with people constantly passing, that I found this very difficult to cope with. The setup for patients was very insensitive.

The psychologist would indicate the area we would work on for the next session. Having geared myself up for this I found that usually she had forgotten.

The one thing I do feel she tried to be was open. She sent for my previous notes, but it took a long time for these to be sent. The psychologist gave me information from these notes which I had never contemplated. She handled it very badly, but I appreciate her telling me. The original GP had said that in his opinion I had fantasied my past and the psychologist he referred me to was inclined to agree. This news was a severe setback and nearly ended in my taking my own life. The psychologist said she would destroy these notes but sadly I have never found out whether she did. She was concerned that I should not challenge these statements, when I hinted I might, as it could get her into trouble, since she should not have shared the information with me. As she could not or would not say she believed me, I felt unable to continue and soon ceased going to further sessions. All she was prepared to say was that it did not matter what she thought. It mattered a great deal, but whether I was right to expect her to commit herself I am unsure. My new GP was very supportive and destroyed his copies of the notes in front of me. He expressed his disapproval of these judgments. Over time I have come to accept that these statements were made in ignorance: the subject of child sex abuse was only just beginning to come out in the open when I first sought help. I will never forget. Even now it hurts a great deal.

By the time I left the services of the NHS I had found my own source of help via a colleague. Previously I had been ignorant about options. I felt in control now and commenced work with a counselor which has proved invaluable.

I have found that I am now more receptive to learning. I went on several short courses at the local college, and no longer found ways to avoid training events related to my work. I began to enjoy these courses and my capacity to learn has increased. This has given me the motivation to undertake training for two years at college . . .

All in all, I have achieved many of the aims on my agenda and this has brought about a much-improved quality of life. It has been a journey of discovery. I don't envisage it having an end and I know for certain the past can never be forgotten, but from the evil deeds of others I have been able to grow and develop in so many ways. Mostly in small things that are usually part of the process of growing up. To me these seemingly small steps have altered my life from existing to living a meaningful life which is interesting and stimulating. My counselor and I achieved it together by the high level of commitment on both sides. I will always be grateful for our time together.

HELEN JONES

# Eating the coal

"Eating the coal" is about oppressions. All of the contributions we received could have addressed the notion of oppression in some way, and many pieces elsewhere in the anthology speak of oppression in direct and indirect terms. The oppressive aspects of silence in "Let healing be the truth" is a demonstration of this point. The authors of this chapter speak about the many forms of oppression they have experienced from others, through the systems and institutions of society, and the ways in which this is compounded and cross-cut by age, gender, disability, sexuality and "race"/ethnicity. "Eating the coal" and "As it was in the beginning," for example, together tackle the dimensions of age, ethnicity and abuse from multiple sources. The following extract from "Refractions" captures the way that dealing with the abuse layers upon other social divisions and expectations; in this case the female being and form:

> I must be pretty,
> I must be thin,
> I must be successful,
> Controlled from within.

We have also included experiences of oppression that are often muted within discussions of oppression. Men's experiences of surviving sexual abuse provide one illustration of this point. Men like Paul, who reminds us that men can be survivors too; or Ron, who resists many of the stereotypical charges that are often leveled indiscriminately at "all men." In "In/out: in/out" Ron describes oppressive and insensitive doctor-patient relationships with which many of us can identify.

Finally here, Gill de la Cour unpacks a number of the complex dilemmas involved in being both a survivor of sexual abuse and a therapist, not only in terms of being able to own her experiences but also in terms of the ways in which, as survivors, we sometimes create our own exclusions by not accepting one another.

———

## Eating the coal

The teacher asked all the children to bring their swimming costume for swimming at the junior school where I had settled after arriving from the Caribbean. With excitement about going swimming I had to ask the woman that spoke with the tongue of a viper for a swimming costume. I was around about eight or nine at the time, and I didn't get one. So I had to watch all the other children splashed around with joy in the pool while I sat on the bench. Water had been a part of my life having grown up with blue radiance of the Caribbean sea, hearing it, seeing it, playing in it every day of my early childhood. I use to cry practically every week when I couldn't go swimming. I asked again and the woman said that I was "stink and dutty," and refused point blank to give me my costume. Those abusive words stuck in my mind. She was my stepmother, a woman who had come into my life on my arrival in England. My natural mother had packaged me off to my father, a former policeman who had come to Britain in 1960. I was around two years old when he left . . .

My skin was forever sore, as daddy was practically beating up on me for the simplest thing. He'd listen to stepmother and her lies every time. These beatings started on the day I arrived in England, and didn't end until I was fifteen years old.

Church music always had an audience inside the house seven

days a week. But I wanted calypso and steel-pan, outside the house I got Mozart and Chopin and Mrs. Walton-Brown's piano.

Poking and topping up the fire in the front room was one of the household duties. In my isolation I reverted to eating the coal from the shed in the back yard. Washing it down with saliva, blackening my gut with jewel from the earth until I was sick. Gorging the plaster from the wall. Sucking the dirt from the potato bag in the cupboard. Then I met Yardley. Yardley, sweet sweet Yardley. The only boy that treated me like I was human, I was sixteen and I think I was in love with Yardley. Stepmother had caught us talking. Just simply talking, it wasn't even in the house either. I had died for Yardley and had come back to life as they pumped the tablets from my stomach in the accident and emergency department and I never did see Yardley again.

Then I was left to find my own way in life. I'd move far away from the area where I was brought up. I was attracted to men unsuitable, who had characteristics that I refuse to put up with. Then I became like a lot of women, I became a single parent.

I was having blackouts. Suffering from agoraphobia and a host of other bits and pieces. I was only twenty-five and felt that I was an old woman of eighty-five. All Doctor R. did was dish out the tranquilizers. Laughing, telling me that it was all in my head when I was there dying in front of his eyes. I got vexed with him, snatched the bloody prescription, took a couple for my shakes and pitched the ten packets in the dustbin. My attitude towards counselors didn't help either. Cos in the back of their tiny minds, all black women were mad anyway. I didn't want to be labelled as mad because I wasn't mad. From there I began a journey of doctoring myself with my own brews.

Then one day I couldn't get out of bed. It was if my brain flipped and had a clean out. Pictures of my early childhood came shattering across my world. I'd started asking questions. Why was I in this blessed place they called England? Why did my mother give me away? Transported me from a comfortable lifestyle to a host of demons along the triangular route of my Atlantic passage on the *Queen Anne*? Then I remembered holding hands going down the alley with my brother and his friends. Rage brewed without no lamentation, as I got angrier and angrier. I hated god, my mother and the family that dragged me up.

For me to sort out my life I had to fly to the island of my birth. At twenty-nine years old I'd met my mother who had relinquished her right as a mother. Who didn't care whether I'd swam or sank. Cos it all started from there. All I got was half-truths and that daddy wanted me. That was her reason for sending me, she said, and she didn't help with my emotional state. Still no answers to the questions I was asking. I came back to England a broken woman.

I was at college doing a course in audio typing and word processing, when I met Juliet, who had moved down to London from Manchester. I was thirty-two and she was thirty-seven. It was like a great load was lifted from my shoulders, and hers as well. We talked about the man who had interfered with her when she was a child in Jamaica. She was very supportive when I talked to her about my rape as a seven-year-old in the Caribbean. She was looking for Jesus and I was looking for revenge. With vengeance I had to confront my father through my aunt who I never turn to as a child. She had so much power and I was petrified of her.

My mother knew all along and hushed up everything, and it took me three months to come out of the shock of her actually knowing. When I'd confront her with my letters to the Caribbean she refused to acknowledge I ever existed, let alone my pain that I had suffered over the years. All the elders knew about my defilement at the time. Mother decided to post me to England and hide it all, but covered up and sheltered her beloved son. Who stood and watched his three friends do what they did, instead of protecting his own baby sister as he was the eldest child. I was all alone in the yard waiting for someone to come which seems like ages. I'd climbed up on the fence looking for Nanny or anyone that could assure me that they were present. Brother was walking along with his three friends them. He saw me peeping over and I cried to see a familiar face. He'd stoned me to go home but I'd refused to go. So he took me by the hands walked along the ally until we came to someone else's backyard. They were all laughing and I was very happy. They'd started playing a game and I was on the dirt floor. Where they tickled my poom poom with their lingy. I didn't want them to put their lingy in my poom poom. I was screaming and they'd pinned me down more. I later ran home and sat down in a corner sucking my thumb. I wish I could go and kill the lot of them. Daddy had received a damaged child from the Caribbean, and treated me like it was my fault. Instead of helping, my new family made things worse. I had survived where millions wouldn't.

I. ASHUNDIE

---

I remember one lesson where we were asked to draw our family tree. I was completely shocked by this, I felt sick and panicky. I could not draw my family tree—it was far too complicated. There were ten children and five different fathers, two of whom my mother had married and divorced. I didn't know anything about my real father, his history or family and I felt numbed by the experience of trying to do this. In retrospect I felt angry at the tutor for doing this exercise: it was a typically middle-class exercise where the tutor expected us to be able to produce nice neat pictures of who we were and where we came from. She had no comprehension of the damage this exercise could do and there was not enough safety within the session to even begin to explain. So I ended up "opting out" of the session, which made me feel embarrassed and humiliated.

There was another instance where we were doing guided fantasy as a form of relaxation and the tutor asked us to remember a happy moment from childhood. Of course I have got happy memories, but at that time I could not access them. Again I began to panic. My mind went blank, there was nothing I could think of. I left that session feeling quite distressed.

There were many other instances of exercises like this that served to make me feel different and in some way "abnormal." I think that this symbolizes a lot of what is wrong in psychiatry: aspects of one's life are categorized as normal or abnormal and if you have had "abnormal" experiences you are made to feel that you are in some way less of a person.

These experiences and what I believe to be normal reactions to traumatic experiences are then somehow transformed into pathology: you become labelled as ill. If you have a certain set of experiences then this must mean that you have this or that "diagnosis." Within this diagnosis the real person that you are is lost and only your label remains. By staying in psychiatry I realize that some could say that I contribute to the perpetuation of this; however, I believe that as long as I can hang on to my beliefs then I can be of some help to people who are in distress and that I can endeavor to see past the labels and make contact with the whole person, not just the diagnosis.

There was and still is the notion that people who experience mental distress are somehow far removed from the human race and should be treated differently because of this. Hospitals are set up to control and contain these people; they are stripped of their rights and are treated like children a lot of the time. I made it my business to ensure that on the ward where I was in charge of clinical care, people were treated with the respect and care they had a right to expect. This did not go down too well with my boss. He thought that I was too liberal; I even had a battle with him about leaving the ward kitchen unlocked so that people could make themselves a cup of tea when they wanted to!

PENNY

## Let healing be the truth

to deny a person her reality of sexual abuse
to say don't tell or else
to refuse the need to be protected
is torture

is to tell the person with the broken leg
that there was no hit and run driver
that there is no reason for fear
when you force her
on to a shameful tightrope
and say walk without wincing

is to tell
the poisoned child
that poison is just fine
that to vomit is wrong
it makes too much mess
so swallow it
again and again

JANINE GUICE

## Extracts from a letter I sent to my ex-therapist

Dear Dr. X

It is important to me that I let you know how I feel about my therapy
with you, in the hope that I can finally put the experience behind me
and move on.

I would like to ask you why you didn't believe me when I told you
I was sexually abused as a child. I needed to explore my fears, but instead
I felt alone. I was so confused that I even believed your version of real-
ity, and felt that I must be very sick to "imagine" that I was abused.

I needed someone to be there for me, to support me, and to accept what I was saying without getting angry and defensive. I didn't
experience this acceptance with you. Instead, I felt as though I was
wrong to tell you, that I was wasting your time as you weren't interested, and that I should just accept your terms, which was to avoid
topics which you didn't want to talk about.

I have written to you in the hope that it will help me to be free
of some of the destructive after-effects I have experienced from my
experience of therapy with you. Although some of our sessions were
helpful in terms of "symptom management," on balance I think the
negative effects have outweighed anything positive I may have gained.

ANONYMOUS

---

Because doctor is always right and
we're crazy or mental cases or not
worth listening to and need drugs to
keep us quiet and if we say we've
been raped it's our own fault or we
made it up or we're having fantasies
and when we feel bad it's
part of our "illness" not because we've
been abused and oppressed because
abuse doesn't exist and if they shout
at us or call us names it's "therapy"
but if we feel angry or upset we're
being manipulative and because eventually
we may accept that they know best as what
choice do we really have and . . .
for lots and lots of other reasons it
is time to make them accountable and
acknowledge what they have done in
the name of therapy.

ALEX BENJAMIN

## In/out: in/out

*Nurse:*   Drop your trousers and wait for the doctor.
*Doctor:*   Now tell me about the problem.
*Patient:*   I have some anal bleeding and the GP thought I might
have piles.
*Doctor:*   Anything else?
*Patient:*   I thought that you ought to know that I was sexually
abused as a child.
*Doctor:*   So that's why you became a nurse.
*Nurse:*   Up on the bed then, push up your knees and drop your
underpants.

*IN/OUT: IN/OUT: all injected. Patient staggers out and
collapses into bed at home for two days.*

*Follow-up six weeks later*

Doctor:     Any more bleeding?

Patient:    No.

Doctor:     Fine.

Patient:    I just wanted to say that last time I told you that I had
            been sexually abused and I felt that you hadn't taken
            that into account when you examined me.

Doctor:     I made a note of it in your file and anyway it happened a
            long time ago.

Patient:    But it was so severe that I only remembered it ten years
            ago. Do you realize that perhaps one in twenty of your
            patients might have had a similar experience?

Doctor:     Well I can only recollect perhaps two in my whole
            history who have mentioned something similar.

Patient:    I still feel that you didn't take it into account in the way
            you treated me.

Doctor:     Do you know how many patients I have to see? How
            many have we seen today, Nurse?

Nurse:      About thirty.

Doctor:     You can't expect me to spend more time with them all.
            There are a lot of demands on me these days. You
            wouldn't have liked it if you had been kept waiting for
            an appointment.

*IN/OUT: IN/OUT: in/out. Speculum—finger—needle—
penis. IN/OUT: IN/OUT: IN/OUT*

RON WIENER

## Am I an abuser?

I wrote this poem on the way to see a psychiatrist. As an incest survivor voicing allegations made by my child concerning her father I
am not to be believed. In fact the social workers involved worked
with three hypotheses.

1. I have made everything up, including my own abuse.
2. I made everything up except my own abuse.
3. The whole experience of my own childhood abuse was so traumatic
   that I am subsequently suffering from a disassociative disorder.

I was therefore to be interviewed to see whether I had abused my own
child and then made allegations. Alongside this process I was accused
of coaching my child into making allegations.

### Am I an abuser?

I walk along the tunnel of the underground
and see the colors bright and clear.
I wonder what this doctor will make of me
And what he'll truly hear.
Will he see me as a yellow
a bright and sunshined day
or will I be a grey and green
miserably moving on my way
And if I'm purple, orange
or even misty blue
Will this make me sane
in the eyes of you
What of all the suffering
my small, bright child has known
Can you see her colors
of every single hue
Does simple truth and honesty
Shine in colors clear
or is that far too simple
and it's words you need to hear?

The psychiatrist saw the colors, but the struggle still goes on.
I hereby write the fourth and missing hypothesis:

4. This mother has struggled against all odds, most of the professionals and the judicial system to have her child's voice heard.
She is telling the truth. As an incest survivor (who has "come to
terms" with her own abuse) we now need to get off our power
pedestal and listen.

B.W.W.

## I was

once a kept
man, a shackled pet, kept
in peace a child could have leapt,
kept by plag
erism, by stage
managed sleight of hand, from rage,

from railings,
from grass knots, snapped swings,
from rusted poles : from things
of speed and
death on wide roads : and
a barricade of roused land
topped by rails
where steam-shifted tails
dragged freight like stolen entrails.

from the toi
let where, as a boy,
I was approached by a coy
man, a strang
er with a mixed range
of pick-up lines and short change.

DAMIAN ROBIN

Ultimately it is a journey that we survivors have to make of our own choice and make alone, but for far too many men the choice is made so difficult by the lack of help and understanding and support. I hope that as time passes, and through increasing education, more and more men will be able to face up to and conquer their inner demons created by abuse, and force an ignorant society to sit up and take notice of a massive problem in its midst.

Men *can* be victims, men *can* be weak, men *can* cry, men *can* hurt, men *can* be emotional, men *can* be used and still retain their masculinity. It must be made clear that it is *not your fault* if you fall foul of someone who can prey on your weaknesses and exploit them for their own perverted ends. *It is not your fault.*

PAUL

## Men

All men, she spat
Feel through their cock,
Holding it tight.

All men I said
Did not include me.

All men she went on,
Assault me daily
With their dark minds.

All men I said
Did not include me.

All men she continued
Abuse me as whore,
Support one another.

All men I said
Did not include me.

All men she emphasized
Worship their power,
Need to control.

All men I said
Did not include me.

All men she concluded
Destroy what is theirs,
One way or another.

All men I repeated
Did not include me.

I don't think she heard.

RON WIENER

## Earth

The earth cracks:
Underneath is grief.

Underneath is
where young girls are kept
for eating pips
for looking back
for making a mistake.

Dare to lie face down
to push your whole arm in
you might find a ribbon from her hair

a daisy chain
a daisy chain
you might find a tiny scrap
you want to keep
a bee sting
a pebble
a scratch.

She says
I ate the seeds
measured myself out in
gleaming red drops to be
sucked off his fingers
spread open
on his table
like meat for dinner.

She says
I am split open
like soft fruit.

She says
have mercy on me
as I pity him yet.

The earth cracks:
The women walk in and out:
Underneath is grief.

ZETTA BEAR

## Refractions

I pass by a shop window,
Disgusting warped images.
Reflections of a monster,
Struggling in controlled confinement.

Oh the eyes were mine.
The rest a crooked malformation,
An obesely distorted slant,
Of internal judgmental dissection.

I must be pretty,
I must be thin,
I must be successful,
Controlled from within.

So troubled with life.
Who I am, what I want?
My resolve has no basis,
It cannot command.

The Ogre needs more,
An insatiable feast,
For a stomach so guilty,
Tortured and weak.

Magazines threaten, models man-made,
Perverse puddings, diets and dates,
Chocolate forbidden
Tempting as fire
Burning, twisting,
Seduction
Desire.

HELEN MARY TREASURER

For the human heart endures much
but can't live in its iron bands forever
Suddenly it flares up like a dying star
anger gushing energy in a shower of fire.

(Ferenc Juhasz)

My father was that most awful of human beasts—an unemployed
married alcoholic. It certainly wasn't my choice or fault to be dogged
with such misfortune, although it seemed that way for a long time.
The "will never drink after marriage" promise had long been broken
and forgotten when I first made contact with the planet in 1958. I am
certain, in hindsight, that I was wanted by both parents, although in
childhood and later I struggled with doubts that my family were indeed my family. Like the society in which I lived, I was blind and ignorant of the ways in which alcohol could tear apart the moral and
emotional fiber of fundamentally good and virtuous people.

My father had been a farmer, a soldier, a boxer and a survivor.
To me, when young, he was simply an alcoholic and a bastard. His
past was totally irrelevant as I became tuned into his ever-changing
and bewildering present. He was never very loving, although sometimes he would display a cheerful disposition and temperament when
drunk. At other times, he would rage. My mother and I would both
feel the full force of his left hook. No one heard as we defended and
consoled each other from his almighty temper. He retired when assured he had won that battle he had once lost.

By 1963 there were three further child-victims. A decision was
made that the family was now heavily laden and thus complete. We
had all "slept" in a large bedroom until the arrival of my third sister.
Now, bedroom positions were to be rearranged and my mother and
father separated. This geographical form of contraception was to
prove costly to me, as the parental hierarchy deigned that I should
sleep in the same bed as my father, lest he should die in the loneliness of his own anguish and sorrows. I had an internal tantrum, but
failed to verbalize it, lest it meant another beating. It wasn't the last

time I surrendered, without expressed objection, to a highly distressing and absolutely unwanted situation.

He arrived drunk on the first night of the new arrangement and promptly collapsed into deep unconsciousness on the bed. I arose from the bed in the hope that my mother would provide some support and comfort. I knocked on the door of the other bedroom. No response. I knocked again. No response. I knew she—they—were all awake. It was too silent. She was abandoning me. I was the trade-in. Loneliness and rejection shivered right through me. No one was there for me. I was all alone in life and I was five years old. I wanted to cry, but couldn't. He might awaken, then Mamma would be angry too. I quietly slid back to bed and stared vacantly into the dark until I lost consciousness.

The sexual abuse began fairly soon after the new relocation arrangements. Invariably, my father was drunk. He would arrive home, usually slobbering, ranting and much given to self-glorification. If I was lucky, he would fall into a deep slumber on entry into bed. Often, he would sing from his repertoire of three songs and would jostle me, attempting to engage me (as though I were a fellow drunk) in his inebriated revelry. Sometimes these music sessions lasted until the small hours and usually were followed by his being "playful" with me. He would tickle my stomach and around the genital area. This always confused me, as I enjoyed the tingly sensations. However, when he went nearer the genitals, I wanted him to stop, but couldn't muster any resistance. He was all-powerful. I was a little boy. I did not recognize that my physical, emotional and other boundaries were being invaded without my consent. Worst of all, I had no one to turn to with my dilemmas and pain. I had a sensation that something untoward was happening, but parents cannot be wrong in a child's eyes. Hence, I took on board the guilt of my father's actions.

Inside, I felt a lot of anger and rage, but was powerless to express it or to stop him. My feelings of shame, self-blame, confusion and self-rejection ensured that my traumas remained firmly in my own head, never to be divulged to another. Sometimes I would

waken to find him masturbating and rubbing his wet penis against my
bum (I had no underwear or pajamas). Other times, I would awaken
to feel something sticky and wet on the bed sheets. Over a period of
time, I began to lie on the very edge of the bed trying to sleep on my
front, so he could only touch my genitals by directly moving my body.
I have no recollection of him attempting overt sexual abuse. My defensive and strained posture has led to long-term problems with my
back.

Often, I had school the following day and was constantly bleary-
eyed and in a state of trance in the classroom, through lack of sleep
and constant anxiety and tension. Even when sexual abuse didn't happen at night, the threat was always there. I was under constant stress.
We slept in the same bed until I was fourteen and physically powerful
enough to assert my right to sleep in an unoccupied ("haunted," my
parents used to tell us children) bedroom. The abuses continued spo-
radically throughout this period.

Soon after the sexual abuse began, my mother also began using
me as a scapegoat and male replacement for her anger against my father. Many times, she beat me with a two-inch-thick, eight-inch-
long stick across the legs and arms for the slightest "mistake." I refused to cry, because I knew it frustrated her and also knew her anger
was being misdirected on to me. She often commented on how "awful" a child I was and how unfortunate she was to be cursed with such
"evil" offspring.

I was smoking with maternal consent and supply at the age of
seven. At about the age of eleven I began drinking alcohol. Because
my financial status was next to nil, I embarked on a career of breaking and entering various premises, to acquire alcohol and cigarettes.
This was fairly common for young people in the area. The estate was
the Council's dumping site for all manner of social misfits. It was impossible to get a job. The area had a reputation and the police wouldn't
come on to the estate after the fall of darkness.

My pain was more acute when I was sober, so I felt the need to
drink more often. Without alcohol, I was easy pickings for social
predators. My esteem was nil and I was uncontrollably emanating sig-
nals that my boundaries could be easily smashed with no consequence to the perpetrator. Consequently, I was on the receiving end

of many uninvited street beatings. My expectations of life were abuse. Between the ages of eleven and fourteen I was sexually violated by two male teenagers from the area. At the age of fourteen I was making regular visits to the GP, who was prescribing Ativan to me "for nerves." I had had numerous overnight stays in police stations and had made several court appearances. I believe I was a fully fledged alcoholic at the age of seventeen.

In March 1984 I met a member of Alcoholics Anonymous, who managed to reach behind my defenses by opening up about himself. I wanted to stop drinking and drugging and had reached the stage where I couldn't from my own resources. So his entry into my life was timely. Coincidentally, within a week I met a new female psychiatrist at the clinic. She decided that I had been on major tranquilizers for far too long and gave me a final six-month prescription. Though stopping drinking, drugging and psychiatry were major blows to my "security" at the time, I now see two people demonstrating a lot of faith in my ability to heal and recover.

Early in 1991 I had almost lost all hope when I came across a book called *Male Rape* in a charity shop. It was my second major brush with good fortune, following my discovery of AA. On reading this book, I began to see very clearly that I had been sexually abused. It seemed that every non-alcoholic idiosyncrasy I had was mentioned and it could all be tied in with being a victim of sexual assault. My heart leapt. A help line was advertised in the back pages and I hoped it was still in operation. I rang at the earliest possible time, got a response and soon was receiving one-on-one specialized sexual abuse psychotherapy.

The one-on-one sessions continued for about six months. Then I was encouraged to join a facilitated group of male survivors. After a further six months, the facilitator departed. I still attend this group once a week and gain valuable support, insight and perspective on my various life situations.

My faith and trust in human beings is increasing daily and my sense of personal safety is getting stronger. I have always felt like a sitting duck and a target for various forms of attack. I exuded victimhood. Over the past few years I am gradually feeling stronger in myself, developing better self-assertion and belief and am more capable of self-protection.

Because most of my healing and recovery has been freely given, involving self-help agencies and the voluntary sector, I am now heavily involved in voluntary activities. I write articles for various newsletters with local and national distribution. I am particularly engaged in the area of mental health. I campaign locally for services for victims of sexual abuse and other forms of oppression. I am fortunate to be on many local forums and committees where my voice is heard and respected, although not always acted upon in ways I would like. However, I feel I have helped to shift the focus somewhat in the planning and delivery of local services for people with mental health difficulties. I enjoy this work, as my own personal experiences and skills combine to at least try to improve services. I also get to meet professionals, whom I used to fear and dread, on an equal basis. I am gradually losing my feelings of inconsequence and inferiority through participation in society on a basis I favor.

RICHIE B.

## As it was in the beginning

War broke out and Dad was called up as he was a British subject. We all moved back to Glasgow by now, Mother and her three children. We moved into a single end with an inside toilet. I would be about seven years old. Mum started drinking and going out most nights, leaving me to take care of the two young ones. I got used to it and was quite the little housewife and mother, a role I very quickly got used to and enjoyed.

Remembering we all slept in one large room, she had a screen round her fold-down bed and we three kids slept in what they called in those days a built-in bed. Our home was very clean, mostly done by myself as she slept all day. I didn't get a lot of schooling, but I loved cleaning the house and taking care of the young ones.

Things were soon to change for the worse. She began to bring the men home. Two men every night most weeks. These men were members of Her Majesty's forces. I won't state what regiment as it wouldn't be right, but she always had a thing about the uniform. She got more money by bringing home two at a time. As she was in bed behind the screen with one, I had to entertain the other one.

I was aged eight and a half by now. I also want to state I was never raped but I was instructed to do sexual acts to these men and let them do likewise to me. If I refused, I was severely punished when they left, as it meant Mother got less money, and I was punished on many occasions I can tell you. It's only a few years since I've been able to sleep in the dark, for one punishment was being put in the coal cupboard which was pitch black and had rats in it. I also got beaten with a carpet beater, my head put under a cold tap, and the tips of my fingers burned. So needless to say, it was not long before I stopped saying "no" to anything I was told to do. I was terrified of my mother and feel ashamed of the hate I felt for her. More so in later years as I grew older.

The abuse continued, and my mother had four illegal abortions. I had to assist, in running back and forward with boiling water and old bits of sheet to clean up. Everything was burned in the open fire that I had to keep going with wood and what they called briquettes in those days. Some time after that, she gave birth to a lovely boy, whom I loved dearly. She wouldn't have much to do with him as he was born with no nose because she caught some illness from the men. She wouldn't take him out because of his deformity, but I took him out in his pram with a small white veil over his face. I hit out at kids who made fun of him, but he died when he was five. For some time after that she brought no men to the house. That is when she started to abuse me. She told me how much she hated me, and if it hadn't been for me she wouldn't have had to marry my father.

For a long time after that, I had to do things she wanted me to do to please her or those awful punishings would start again. I dreaded when I was demanded to get into bed with her. I hated the abuse with the men friends, but this was worse. Often I was sick after it, but got no compassion—just warned what I would get if I told anyone. After some months she started going out for men again as money was scarce. So it all started over again—abuse by men—and it continued with her through the day . . .

STEPHANIE MCGUIRE

## Cannibal Docks article one

All stand for the Man in wig and frock.
Woman-in-the-dock, place your hand
upon the phallus, swear to speak
the Facts, the Hard Facts, nothing but
the Facts of Life your Father taught you.
Do you know the Law?

*I know the lore of my own land—*
*you call it Nightmare—its dialect*
*is one you may not understand.*

Please instruct
your witness to speak clearly,
or her evidence
may be dismissed.

*I learned your language on my father's knee,*
*its smack and hiss and whistle,*
*Come near to me,*
*and I'll instruct you now to listen*
*with an unpricked ear.*

Ah! You have an impediment, my dear?
Let me reassure—
aliens, barbarians, all
whose speech is queer
are equal in a court of law.
Proceed by telling us what you recall.

*I know that I ate my father's penis,*
*to save my life,*
*when I was small.*

How small?
What exactly happened?

When?
What time of day?
What age, precisely,
were you then?
Who else was there?

*I was alone,*
*and small,*
*and bare.*
*He—*
*was very large.*
*And hard.*
*My mouth is soft.*
*And wide as a consequence.*
*I bellow from the corners,*
*flex my tongue*
*around the pillar established there.*
*You think me dumb*
*but I am adept in—*
*a vulgar lore.*

Are you quite sure
you understood the question?
Did you say you were a victim
of abuse?

*I say I am*
*a cannibal.*
*Since I ate my father's rod for breakfast*
*when a child,*
*I have a singularly muscled jaw,*
*and have grown long and sharp*
*in tooth.*
*I have an appetite for power*
*and a stomach for the most unpalatable*
*truth.*

Can you prove this to us?

*Bear with me while I lift your skirt, my lord,*
*expose the staff on which your honor rests,*
*stiff test of truth,*
*hard, upright, evident,*
*your measuring rule,*
*your judgment's thrust,*
*your punishing sentence-stick*
*Let this scaffold stand on its own merits,*
*so to speak.*
*Article One for public view—*
*Can you see it from the gallery? Look closely!—*
*I will demonstrate my art with relish,*
*just for you.*

RUNA WOLF

## Whose reality are you living?

I first became interested in the difference between facts and the truth when writing autobiographical accounts of my experience of so-called mental illness. For me, "recovery" was a process of redefining those experiences, rejecting the medical labels, and finding new words to express what I had been through. Coming to terms meant coming to my *own* terms, and thereby regaining some dignity and a sense of a continuous, rational self.

As I wrote, my accounts diverged more and more from my official medical case history. The facts were the same—dates of admission to hospital, numbers of ECT treatments, details of self-woundings, suicide attempts, a series of diagnoses—but the *truth* that I was searching for (you might say, creating for myself) involved some sort of *interpretation* of these facts, an *explanation* that assumed I had had a good reason for behaving the way I did.

What disturbed me most, during this process, was not the divergence of my account from that of the experts (others were also rejecting the experts at the time, even turning insanity into political rebellion or mystical enlightenment) but the way my *own* interpretation kept changing. Could I never fix the truth about my past? How many pasts could one person have? How could I tell which version (if any) was the true one?

But the real crisis came several years later, when I thought I had put the mental illness issues "behind me." Without realizing it, I had for five or six years been hiding the full story of my past from others and minimizing it in my own mind, in order to "pass" as a fully functioning, if rather vulnerable, "normal" member of society. Then I began to have nightmares about rape. At first, the dreams were of a man trying to break into my house, me frantically trying to bolt doors and windows, waking in terror just in time, before . . . Increasingly, in this repeating scenario, there was a sickening sense that the man was someone I knew, and there would be a child in the house—my child—who I was terrified I would not be able to protect.

Then, in a particularly harrowing one, I was an amnesiac, fighting off the realization that I had committed an unforgivable crime, one for which I would be boiled in oil. Then running, in night clothes, through the streets, looking for my father to protect me, my father drawing me into his house for safety, my father sitting on my bed, my father . . . *the man I was trying to escape from.*

I had wondered before, when hearing survivors of sexual abuse describe their experiences, whether I too had been abused, but had dismissed this notion because I could not remember any such thing. I had always been frightened of my father, repulsed by him physically, and had had a difficult life, including a lot of problems with sexuality. But basically, I thought my parents, though inadequate in some ways, were decent people. I knew my problems originated in childhood, but blamed myself, and mental health professionals, for my having taken so long to "get over" them.

When the nightmares had reached the pitch where I felt devastated for days after each one, I asked myself in earnest whether I could have been abused by my father. I went into a state of deep shock which lasted several months. Could it be true? I never doubted that the perpetrator, if there was one, was my father. Somehow I knew in my very bones that this whole issue was about him. I became obsessed with the idea, immobilized by it, haunted by it hour after hour. Eventually, worn out, I shelved the question, telling myself that if I had been abused it did not really matter. It was a long time ago, my parents were old now, and I would never know for sure . . .

But the idea returned with a vengeance exactly a year after the nightmares had begun, and this time I found the courage to follow it through. Breaking contact with my parents turned out to be the key to uncovering the truth. I could not open up the horror of my past while trying to hang on to the illusion of loving parents in the present.

Eventually I gave up my job to engage fully in the process of therapy. My parents, my brother, and for a time, my younger sister (who I know now was also abused) denied my "disclosures," effectively rejecting me from the family. The almost overnight loss was devastating. In such a short time to lose my family, to have to reconstruct my whole personal history, to re-examine everything I thought I knew about the world, was overwhelming. I had no energy left for anything else. I was swamped by grief. The rage came later. And finally, much later—excitement, transformation, triumph, calm.

So now I have this new version of my past. I still have no clear-cut memories, no visual information, nothing verifiable from the outside. Yet I *know* I was abused. Apart from my family, those who know me have never doubted me. I have relived the abuse, horrifically, many times in therapy. I remember it physically and emotionally, if not visually, and that is good enough for me.

It explains everything—my bizarre sexual awareness from early childhood, my gender-identity confusion, desperate sexual experiences with men, acts of self-mutilation, the so-called mental illness—it makes sense of my past in a way no other "interpretation" has done.

But what does all this imply about what is real, about how we arrive at the truth? My parents and my Anglican vicar brother still vehemently deny my allegations. I have no proof, other than the evidence of my life's experiences, my emotions, my dreams, my body-memories—in other words, my *self*, my sense of *who I am*. These things, which are everything to me—my integrity, my humanity—are they, in the face of a lack of hard evidence, enough?

Not for a court of law. Not for those who prefer to think that parents, simply by virtue of being parents, have some greater access to reality than their offspring. Not for those experts who have manufactured the false memory syndrome and concocted, like witch-hunters of the past, a conspiracy of therapists out to bring the family to its knees.

But my own truth is more than good enough for me. There is a choice. Not to believe in my self means I am either a vicious liar, a complete fool, or mentally ill. I know I am none of these. And since I placed my trust firmly in my own version of the past, my present world has changed. In place of an isolated alienhood, a toehold in the normal world I wanted so badly to accept me, I have both feet firmly planted and am much taller and infinitely more capable than I realized.

So have I fixed the truth about my past now, written the definitive life story? I am sure I have not. My past will continue to change as my understanding of my self continues to grow. Maybe more memories of abuse will return, maybe other aspects of my childhood will assume greater significance. But this prospect no longer worries me. What I know now is that facts (dates, witnessed events, evidence that will stand up in court) are no more related to the truth than a railway timetable is to the experience of a journey.

The past that matters is not "out there" but inside of me, my inner reality, the foundation of the me that I experience in the present, and project into the future. This inner reality is a dynamic, creative process, not an object which can be pinned down, trapped in time to form a single eternal truth. Trusting this process liberates creative powers and sharpens perception. It is not a hazy, anything-goes, believe-what-you-like fantasy world, but a gathering of the senses, the intellect, the intuition into one powerful focus of awareness—it is being "I," the author of my own existence, furnishing my world with the meanings and values which I have carefully chosen. It is being alive, it is being human in the profoundest sense. Anything less is a self-mutilation, however subtle or invisible.

I believe now that "the truth" is always a personal choice, an act of faith—no less for my parents or the false-memory experts than for me. You have to decide, to make a commitment. Will you believe the denying parents who claim that simply because they were the grown-ups at the time they must be telling the truth now? (Because parents inevitably define the world for us when we are dependent children, do they still have the right to do so when we are grown?) Will you put your trust in "facts," in the sort of evidence that law courts demand, in psychological theories about memory based on scientific research? Or will you dare to listen to the truth embodied in a nightmare, to accept the evidence of an adult body in the throes of a remembered rape, to recognize the logic of a reconstructed life-story, to trust that deep intuitive knowledge, that gut conviction of what is right?

It's a frightening, risky business. Our culture has a very limited idea of what counts as real, has vested the power to define reality in a masculine minority for whom "science," the experts, are often the spokespeople, the PR merchants. They will always have an answer—a new syndrome or complex, backed up by research, statistics, evidence—to every challenge to their monopoly on reality. It's no good waiting for "the truth" about childhood sexual abuse to be untangled "out there," or for your own memory to provide a neatly packaged set of facts which at last no one will be able to dispute. When it comes to the fabric of our own lives, the basis of our identity, our Selves, we have to be our own experts. We each of us have to decide how to recognize the truth, how to define and name reality. At the heart of the question "what is true?" is the more fundamental issue: whose side are you on?

RUNA WOLF

---

She wanted to give me something, something I could hold on to, so she told me I was strong.

I would like my head to be full of fluffy kittens lapping whipped cream. Instead I have piranha fish lurking in treacle. I would like to be as soft and bendy as still water on a scorching summer day. Instead I am as tight as a tower block in the middle of the city.

I am strong. What other choice have I had? But it has come with a price I can't name because it makes me cry too hard to think about it. It has come because the only other option I could ever see was to die. My body could die, I know my spirit is clawing to hold on right now, and parts of me have already died.

Strong is making me die.

If you want to give me something, hear me, don't put me out there alone. Take my hand, give me yours, and let's go make a world where we don't have to be strong.

FRANCESCA GARLAKE

J.K. HORN

(Women's Forest)

## Survivor or expert? Some thoughts on being both

I am a professional counselor working with clients who have experienced sexual abuse as children. I am also a "survivor" myself. When I was very young, I was sexually abused by a man who was, apparently, a close family friend. The abuse was extreme and traumatic. The way my family operated ensured that the experience was covered up and denied. The resulting feelings and terrors I suffered were consequently never acknowledged or dealt with during my childhood. It is only now I am an adult that I have been able to work through some of my feelings within the safety of my own personal therapy. I am an expert and a survivor; I have a foot in both camps. However, in this article I would like to question the validity of the very notion of these two camps and to examine what may be the significance of such polarized thinking, where this area is commonly perceived as consisting of two mutually exclusive groups.

The tendency to divide this area into work done by experts and work done by survivors themselves could be understood as the result of "splitting." In psychoanalytic theory, the process of splitting is seen as a primitive form of defense against overwhelming and unbearable fears and impulses. Melanie Klein has argued that the infant perceives the world in split terms of "good breast" and "bad breast," attributing to the bad breast all its own sadistic impulses and images of persecution and attack. This process serves the purpose of allowing the infant to disown such feelings, as they are seen to belong to something outside, to something "other." Unfortunately, once this has happened, the outside embodiment of these projected feelings becomes an extreme persecutor as it has been filled with all that is too unbearable to be contained within. Although this mechanism of defense originates from such an early stage of development, it is available to us and operative throughout our lives on both an individual and group basis. In short, we all do it!

Groups of any size will often use splitting to attribute fearful and destructive impulses to an outside enemy, thereby sparing themselves the painful task of owning, exploring and making reparation for destructive feelings which exist within. Such a mechanism is most likely to be used in situations which arouse a threatening level of anxiety. Childhood sexual abuse is obviously one such extreme and has consistently been responded to with the defenses of splitting and denial.

This process can operate on a huge and sometimes obvious scale. While writing this, I am struck by the ironic image of the crowds which gathered around the police van transporting the two boys found guilty of murdering and stoning James Bulger: the irony being that the crowd showed its anger and revulsion by hurling stones at the escorting police van. Splitting can also operate in a far more insidious and subtle form which colors and influences our relationships, our work and our ways of thinking. While the very reasoning behind the concept of this anthology results from the history of the way in which sexual abuse has previously been viewed, reacted to and written about, it also reflects an apprehension of reality which results from conscious and unconscious splitting.

By this process, "experts" working with survivors will often deny their own survivor within. In such a divided world of us and them, we the experts are the ones who analyze, research and suggest treatment for our clients: it is only they outside who have such problems, it certainly is not us. Thus the outside group of clients/patients/survivors can be abused again unwittingly and apparently for their own good while the experts disown the fact that they may share difficult feelings and experiences. At one extreme a survivor attempting to communicate pain and distress through symptoms of life-threatening anorexia may be force-fed and rendered powerless. More commonly and pervasively, the survivor may be abused again in a far more subtle way by being generally doubted, feared, blamed and treated with disrespect. In the world of us and them, there is a powerful unconscious assumption at work that the two groups are mutually exclusive. So it is possible for a fellow professional to refer a client to me with an offensive remark like: "Well, you know what it's like with these survivors, they often repeat the patterns of abuse with their own children. We're very worried about her baby . . ."

Such a remark could only be made to me by someone assuming that as I am a professional, therefore I cannot possibly be a survivor myself. The assumption that the problem belongs to "that lot out there" is so pervasive and strong and the shame and stigma of abuse so great that the survivor within (and here I am clearly referring to myself) is gagged into silence. So far, under these circumstances, I have not been able to declare myself as not only one of us but also one of them too.

However, the survivor group can also fall into this same trap of split thinking. It is easy to see how this can happen around an issue which produces such high levels of fear and anxiety. While the Kleinian bad breast becomes an arch-persecutor embodying our disowned destructive impulses, the Kleinian good breast embodies our hopes and aspirations. Unfortunately this also represents a distorted reality, as over-idealization can at best lead to disappointment and at worst provoke profound envy and confirm a sense of our own impoverishment and worthlessness. Clients often come into counselling with the conscious or unconscious assumption that they are coming to see someone who is psychologically perfect and flawless. Since a counselor should not disclose their own material for many reasons, not least because the session is sacredly reserved for the client's needs and material, such an assumption would be largely unchallenged. Clients entering into counselling and psychotherapy are in a highly vulnerable position and so may need to believe that the person in whom they are placing their trust has greater expertise and is more perfect in every way than they are themselves. On the other hand, such vulnerability may provoke the opposite reaction and a client may need to rubbish their counselor with the "what would she know about it anyway" type of response. Clients may also have the need to believe that they have an untarnished-by-abuse professional to help them. A survivor who is going through the painful struggle of overcoming feelings of guilt and shame may need to avoid even the thought that their counselor may be "tarred with the same brush." The admonition, "Physician heal thyself!" has deep roots and reverberations.

In order to be a non-damaging and effective counselor, all professionals owe it to themselves and their clients to be in a continual process of developing self-awareness and actively working on their own areas of personal difficulty through training and therapy. However, if we had our difficulties so well and easily resolved as to be psychologically perfect, then we would have very few feelings of genuine empathy with our clients. On the other hand, if we are so damaged by unresolved feelings that we take these out on our clients, then we will lack the objectivity to be able to offer the lack of fear and the impartiality which can be so helpful. As professionals we need to offer the genuine emotional response which comes from having experienced painful struggles of our own while at the same time being able to offer a dispassionate analysis which can provide our clients with safety and clarity. Furthermore, while I am working with a survivor I am always aware that their material and reactions may be utterly different from my own, even though I know that we share the experience of having been abused.

While there is a strong external reality which has given an historical need for the survivor to speak out in their own voice, to be their own expert, and to claim their own feelings, this may nevertheless be complicated by the distortions of an internal reality where unhelpful defenses are at work. Personal change and development can be a disorientating and threatening experience. We often cling to what we know best. If we know how it feels to be held by the anguish of isolation, rage and despair and to relate to others with profound mistrust, then we may view the world in such a way that these feelings are perpetuated. Such patterns are not our fault and result from something that happened to us in the past but that may not be happening to us in the present. It may be possible to relinquish old and limiting ways of perceiving and relating in favor of new ways which, although more confusing, are more open and enriching. The world could indeed be more grey than we (survivors and experts alike) assume and far less black and white.

I therefore suggest that survivors may also be guilty of an "us and them" split in the same way as experts. I once had the salutary experience of being emotionally attacked at a meeting by a representative from a women's survivors' group. As I was seen at the time to be in the expert camp, she made the assumption that I could not possibly know anything meaningful about sexual abuse. She saw me only as a professional counselor and to her this meant that I couldn't have the benefit of any first-hand experience. The setting would have been utterly inappropriate for any personal disclosure on my part and so I was unable to challenge the assumptions behind the exchange between us.

Until recently, I have unconsciously believed that these two groups are mutually exclusive and that I am guilty of some form of transgression by secretly belonging to both. Perhaps I am guilty of some dreadful act of duplicity by having a foot in each camp? I am still beset by fears that most survivors will recognize. Who should I tell? Who can I trust with this shameful secret and this double act? I must admit that it is far more comfortable for me to be seen as solely aligned with the professionals: that persona carries status, not stigma. Anyone I tell of my secret may imagine that I'm bound to abuse or collude with the abuse of my children. Similarly they may have fears that I'll abuse my clients. On a very deep level, I have these fears myself. As a counselor, I may damage my clients; as a client I may manipulate my therapist into abusing me. The psychoanalytical precept that we all tend to repeat patterns of behavior is loaded when it comes to abuse because of all the stigmatization and fear of contamination which are involved.

Sometimes it is possible to learn a great deal by reminding ourselves of the obvious, so I'll state the obvious here. Being a person involves being more than any one thing. I am both a mother and a daughter. I am both a survivor working on my own pain in therapy and a counselor undertaking therapeutic work with survivors. The assumptions of my colleagues and clients; the collective myths and fears of our society and my own feelings and fears of shame fuse together to make this a most uncomfortable and uneasy combination. But there is hope. As a trained and experienced professional, I have a wider view than that which could be gained purely from subjective experience. As a survivor I have real experience of how all this feels with an immediacy which could not possibly be learned from theoretical understanding alone. In both groups I feel different. In some ways, and especially on bad days, this can feel like being the odd one out and is upsetting. In other ways though, I know we are all different from each other anyway and working with difference can be the source of great creativity and growth.

I will conclude with the most crucial and painful dilemma that has emerged while writing this article. Can I own who I am? Can I let clients and colleagues identify this struggling double agent? What I am wrestling with, of course, is whether or not to sign my name. Perhaps this feels like "coming out." I am unsure whether I am more afraid of my own feelings or of other people's stereotypes and assumptions that may get dumped on me. I am afraid of the stigma which I know still surrounds survivors of sexual abuse. Why should I continue to feel ashamed of being a survivor? I would have no dilemma to work through if this article only showed me as an expert and I'm sure I would readily sign my name to it then! If I don't sign this, then fear will be compelling me to disown my survivor within. If I do sign, I'll be saying that this struggle has been mine and I'm proud of how far I've come with it. I will be acting on my rational belief that the two groups are not mutually exclusive and that it is possible to be both. I can own all of who I am. I can be proud of being me.

GILL DE LA COUR

## I didn't want to grow up like this

I look in the mirror and don't see me
but someone I can't even bear to see,
a body distorted and overweight,
a woman I simply abhor and hate.

When I was young, I had different thoughts,
I excelled at school and was good at sports.
I had no plans to be me. Instead,
I vaguely visualized life ahead:

University, then a life of bliss?
Not really, but I didn't imagine this;
for the violent abuse when I was four
meant life had different plans in store.

The injury incest had done to me
grew into bone that became TB.
And years of hospitals and doctors induce
further pain and add more abuse.

Four years I lay in a rigid frame
because my father had played that game.
Then, doubly crippled, in body and mind,
I tried to transmute it and leave it behind.

But, when I look in a mirror now,
I see with shock what it's done, and how
I've grown up ugly and twisted and fat.
I didn't mean it to be like that.

BRENDA NICKLINSON


## Paranoia

I open the cupboard, he is there
I look in the mirror, he is there
I go to the shops, he is serving me
I go on the bus, he sits beside me
I go for a walk, he comes with me
I pick up the phone, I hear his voice
I read a book, his name appears,
I watch TV, he is reading the news out
I listen to music, he sings the songs,
I have a shower, his presence is there
I make my lunch, he stands by the cooker,
I make a cup of tea, he puts the kettle on
I get ready for bed, he watches me
I get into bed, he follows me.

MARGARET ANN TAYLOR

## A letter I wrote after seeing my GP
## who wanted me to see a psychiatrist and
## I didn't want one

I just wanted to tell you, I don't need a psychiatrist. Whatever you may think, I know I don't. I don't need someone to say sort yourself out, you shouldn't be like this. Tell me why? Am I supposed to be happy-go-lucky, cheerful, when I remember in detail how my childhood ended. When I look back and see in childhood I was being made to do things that I should never even have known about. Maybe I am depressed, or maybe I'm grieving for my childhood, the childhood stolen from me. Those years when I should have been playing, but instead was an adult in a child's body. I need to do this with support and encouragement, not from a shrink who has knowledge from books. Don't tell me it's not too bad or hard when you've never known it. It's been nearly a year now, yet four years were taken from my body. So, if it takes that long, so be it, but I don't need a psychiatrist. If I had to see one, my career would be over and I'd be worse than I am now.

As for these tablets you've given me, I thought I wanted them and needed them, but now I've got them, I don't want them. They can sit on my shelf because I don't want to be seen in such a state and my abuser walk away from all harm.

SARAH

ONE DAY MY SISTER'S MOUTH
GOT STUCK OPEN.

THE PSYCHIATRIST SAID,

THAT IT (WAS NO MEMORY
        OF THE PENIS IN HER
        MOUTH WHEN SHE WAS 3)
WAS A PSYCHOTIC EPISODE.
HE ALSO SAID THAT HER HAND AND ~~FOOT~~
FEET MOVEMENTS, WHICH NEVER
STOPPED + UPSET HER GREATLY,
HAD NOTHING WHATSOEVER TO
DO WITH THE MASSIVE DOSE OF
    DRUGS HE FORCED ON HER.

JANINE GUICE

JANINE GUICE

## The court case

My story began in 1964; I was four and a half. My father sexually abused me from that time until early 1977. There were other abusers, who were my father's friends. It felt like I was only born for that purpose.

My mother was also an abuser: she would always be under the influence of alcohol, as was my father.

I was always told by my father that it was my fault and if I told anyone I would be locked away. And of course I believed him. He would threaten me with beatings, and even death.

Until two years ago I lived with my past. It was my secret. My father's mother died when I was away on holiday. By the time I came back home she had been buried. I was sad that I was unable to say goodbye. I rang various aunts and uncles to convey my condolences. One aunt said she thought that she knew why I did not visit very often. I asked her what she meant, but she wanted me to tell her.

So with that I started to tell her my story, hoping that she would believe me. And to my surprise she did. In fact she told me that my father had done things to her. It was a relief to me that she did believe me.

A few weeks after the phone call my aunt invited me up to Scotland for the weekend. There I met my father's brothers, sisters, their husbands and wives. They listened to part of my story, but stopped me halfway through, as they had heard enough to know what had gone on. They also believed me; it was a great relief.

On the following day my cousin, who is in the police force, came to see me, and he suggested that I go and speak to the Female and Child Protection team. I took his advice, and went along the next day. I was taken into an office where the phone was ringing on and off and where people were coming in and out.

So here was I coming out with some powerful emotions with all this going on in the background.

As far as I was concerned I was only there to offload my feelings, and I was aware that the policewoman was writing things down. I was there for four hours and at the end of that time I was mentally and physically worn out. I said to the policewoman that I would go home and think about what I had said, to which she replied that it was out of my hands and that they were going to take it as far as they could.

Because my father was in the Army the abuse took place in Scotland, England and abroad, which meant that other police forces became involved. I first went to Scotland in September 1992, yet it was not until January 1993 that the police from North Yorkshire rang me and said that they would have to come out and take another statement, as the one that I gave in Scotland was no good to them. So a date was fixed, and a policewoman from North Yorkshire came to my house. She could not apologies enough. She was appalled that the Scottish police had not taken enough care when taking my statement.

My next statement took from nine in the morning until eight in the evening to finish. When I read my first statement I could see the need for the second. In the second statement I had to go into great detail—how far did penile penetration go, what did he say while he was abusing me, was I lying on my left side or my right, dates, was anyone there at the time? It was all very painful but it had to be done.

The policewoman mentioned the Criminal Injuries Compensation Board. At first I was appalled, and said that I was no one's prostitute, but she said, that it did not come out of his pocket, and it was the system's way of saying sorry that it had failed to help.

So after thinking long and hard, after a few months I did fill in a form, which took several painstaking hours. The form was sent off; all I had to do was wait for the reply.

It came in December 1993. This is what it said.

**Applications for compensation will be entertained only if made within three years of the incident giving**

rise to the injury, except that the Board may in exceptional cases waive this requirement.

The Board has always adopted a sympathetic attitude to late claims where the incidents occurred in childhood. The one instance where the Chairman is unable to be flexible is where the incidents occurred prior to 1st October 1979 and where the applicant and the offender were living together as members of the same family. Such cases are bound by the terms of a previous scheme which debarred compensation being paid in these circumstances.

The terms of that scheme continue to apply and regretfully your application to the Board was bound by these terms as the last incident occurred prior to 1st October 1979. In such matters the Chairman's decision is final and there is no right of appeal against the decision not to allow waiver of the limitation period.

I regret that on this occasion I am not able to be more positive.

This new law changed the 1969 Act, so where was I supposed to live as a child of nine?

Now at the age of thirty-four I am going to the Crown Court, as the police are prosecuting my father. It has taken nearly two years to get this far. My case comes up in July. Perhaps justice will be done, but I do not hold out much hope.

But if nothing else I hope that it brings awareness to millions of people in the outside world that this sort of thing does go on and that it is nothing new. And I hope that it may help a lot of other adults that it has happened to, to speak out. It is not our fault that we were bodies without a voice.

I do not pretend that this has been easy; in some ways it has been worse than the abuse itself. When the abuse was happening you knew from day to day what was going on, but with the law as it is today you are left in the dark, until they decide to let you know what is going to happen.

Over the past year I have tried to commit suicide three times, my last attempt being on 3 February 1994. Each time was with tablets. It has taken me until now to realize that he is not worth it. If I was to succeed in killing myself he would have won; at least if I stick around I have a fighting chance—don't I?

The thought of going to court frightens me, but it is something that I have to do. Not only for myself and other people, but for that little four-and-a-half-year-old who was too scared to speak out.

The worst thing for me is having to see that man again. That will be my biggest ordeal—not his defense trying to make out that I am telling lies, since I cannot add or take away anything that I have said in my statements.

I feel that I am the one on trial. After all, the judge and jury are not going to see the little girl or the frightened teenager, but a woman.

I have to consider what to wear, and not wear too much make-up. In other words, do not make myself too attractive, as the jury look very closely at you, and it seems that a lot of these cases go on how you present yourself. I am the sort of person that uses make-up to hide behind; without it I feel that people can see abuse me written on my forehead. That feeling has never left me since I was a child. Maybe it never will.

I am not looking forward to telling my story in court with him sitting there, as I know that he might get pleasure from it. That is the kind of person he is. I will feel naked even though I know that I will have my smart grey suit on; but he strips with his eyes.

So to conquer this feeling I am going to use imagination, I am going to imagine that underneath my grey suit I will be wearing stripy pop socks, a pair of football boots, big baggy shorts and T-shirt with his face on it and an axe going through his head, so that is what he will see if he dares to strip me with his eyes.

At the moment I feel strong, but the case is still a few months away. I only hope my strength continues to grow as it has done these past few months.

This time last year he nearly did win.

But whatever the outcome, no one can ever give me back my virginity. I will never know what having a childhood would be like, and what it is like to have loving, caring parents.

What are a loving mother's and father's arms like? I will never know.

FIONA ELIZABETH REAY, ALIAS KERR

# You want a witness?

---

"You want a witness?" examines, through a rich variety of perspectives, the role that people, institutions and "society" itself play in making it even harder for us to survive and move forward. The contributions in this chapter have in common the fact that the responsibility for child sexual abuse is placed back where it belongs—with the abuser(s) and the "deaf crowd" of society. "Can you hear?" pulls together a number of strands that are addressed by many of the narratives in this anthology. The author talks of the struggle to speak out about the abuse, the struggle to be understood and the struggle to be taken seriously. Being heard, being believed, being cared for and being responded to appropriately are central themes of this chapter. The following lines describe one element of this:

> When we say we were abused by women
> women don't abuse, it's just not so,
> it's all in your head and you must let it go.

"Living in a daydream (FMS—the nineties nightmare)" depicts another element through an ironic view of what it is society wants to hear and the ways in which "nice people" are expected to behave. "Middle-class girls" also reflects this through a direct challenge to the way in which middle-class girls are supposed to live their lives and feel.

Carla, in "O! Social Services," poses a direct challenge to the social services and we would like to extend her invitation to the "deaf crowd" to:

**"PROVE THAT YOU REALLY DO GIVE A DAMN! IF YOU CAN"**

## Mauve blues

### I

The exiled queens and kings of sorrow sing their lavender blues in carpetless hotel rooms. Outside, passing clouds shift their shapes— now a fish, now a dragon, now the face of someone you know—and are unreachable. The children on the green have blown away the dandelions and tossed aside the daisy chains, and are weaving new songs out of nettles and thistles.

### II

I suppose you're expecting to hear what a hard time I have being a sexual abuse survivor. To hear how I sob and rant, rant and sob. How I visit my therapist, support my support group, and hug my teddy. How brave (but tragic) I am. What a splendid testimony I offer to the unsinkable human spirit.

Perhaps, for all that, you find the prospect a little daunting. Perhaps your supplies of sympathy and pity are running a trifle low. Perhaps, indeed, you're beginning to suffer from compassion fatigue. Well, dear reader, have no fear, these won't be the sort of blues. I shan't be calling on your sympathy or your pity. I know what they're worth, and I tell you, you can keep them. In fact, you can shove them.

### III

The other day I was standing in line at a supermarket checkout. It was late afternoon, a busy time. Ahead of me, a well-dressed woman was packing her purchases and sorting out her credit card. She had a

daughter about three or four years old. A graceful, attractive child—
the kind of child who would draw smiles and greetings and compliments. Except that everyone around was making a great effort not to
notice her, as if this child were hidden under a cloak of invisibility.
There seemed to be no good reason for this, apart from the fact that
she had a large and very apparent black eye.

It seems like the only good child abuse victim is a dead one.
Everybody knows what to do then. Check that the child has a birth
certificate. Otherwise, pretend it never happened. Check it was a
good little child and didn't run away from home. Otherwise it can be
a statistic. Check the parents didn't do it. Otherwise blame the social workers. Check someone else did it, and make sure it's nobody
too important, or it wouldn't be in the public interest to prosecute.
And then when all the checks have been checked and double-
checked, have a nice big spontaneous public outcry and wonder if
enough is being done to protect our children.

Because if the child stays alive, then the whole situation becomes rather awkward. Nobody quite knows where to put their face.

In those heady days when I first started to come out as a survivor
of child sexual abuse, I thought my candor would be appreciated, at least
by my friends. I mean, they were always encouraging me to be myself,
be more open, be real. The conversation would go something like this:

*Me:* "My father sexually assaulted me."
*Friend:* "Really . . . and how *is* your father?"

And several times my disclosures of experiences of sexual abuse
have been taken as some sort of confession to harboring perverse sexual proclivities. Friends nod sagely and say "we always thought so,"
and make a mental note not to ask me to babysit for them.

It seems that to speak of sexual violence is not to speak of violence, but to speak of sex. Pain and despair as sub-species of eroticism.

I used to go to a therapy center where the therapists listened at-
tentively while I dug my way into my traumas. Once as I passed by
the staff toilet, its door was standing wide open and a tube of KY Jelly
was in plain view on the washbasin. I think of it as their way of telling

me I wasn't suffering in vain, I was after all bringing a little spice into their lives.

How to avoid that particular degradation, in the therapy room, say, or in the witness-box? Some survivors adopt the strategy of recounting their abuse experiences in as toneless and deadpan a voice as they can muster. But one doesn't get off lightly for being such a spoilsport. One is liable to be accused of having no feelings, of not really minding that one has been sexually assaulted. It takes a while to learn that one isn't here to be understood, one is here to perform.

Maybe we survivors should be grateful, as society solves the problem of what to do with us when we inconveniently stay alive. Give us a career in lifelong humiliation. No need to worry about being made redundant, and we even get the chance to work from home.

A survivor can never be too humble. I discovered this one evening as I was waiting on a tube station platform to change trains. A man approached me, a complete stranger, carrying a rolled-up umbrella, tipped with a metal spike. He playfully made to poke me in the stomach with it. For some reason, I wasn't in my usual placatory mood. Sometimes it's hard to be everyone's round-the-clock pet. I clapped him on the shoulder and said, "Hey, what's your game?" He didn't reply, but very quickly I was on the ground being kicked and striving to protect my face and head. Eventually, someone intervened and the man strolled away. I had a sensation of trying several times to get back into my body. But what surprised me most was the large number of people watching from the platform, and from the open doors of a train that had just pulled in. They were laughing; not all of them, but many of them. Laughing with enjoyment. And I felt as if in those merry faces I had caught a glimpse of England's dark, sardonic heart, and having glimpsed it once, I would see it always, like the sulphury sunlight in the sky.

## IV

Every night, I kneel beside my bed and pray to Jesus. "Jesus," I whisper. "Lucky for you, before they crucified you, you weren't raped into the bargain. They must have been nice, well-mannered lads, those Roman soldiers, who didn't do that sort of thing. Because if you had been raped, nobody would believe in your innocence any more. Your followers wouldn't have greeted your resurrection with open arms, and tears in their eyes; instead, they'd have given each other knowing looks, and digs in the side with their elbows. "Well, well, well," they might have said, with a smirk, "you're a dark horse! A bit of Roman, eh! So now we know."

"People wouldn't tell their children about you. Your story would be strictly for adults. No more "King of Kings" or "St. Matthew Passion" on prime-time television at Eastertide. It would all be late-night viewing and problems with the censors. Certain passages in the gospels would be left untranslated or rendered into Latin. If a young girl coming home from the fields saw a vision of you, and her friends and family asked her what you looked like, she would have to tell them, "I couldn't see his face, it was blurred out—I suppose they have to protect his identity."

"You could have counted the number of your flock on the fingers of one broken hand. The extra stigma would have been too much even for you to bear. You would have felt what it's *really* like to be human. And then you would understand that when you rose from the dead, you weren't the only one."

## V

Good people of England, we interrupt your drive-time hit-show to bring you a newsflash! Elves and goblins are gathering on your doorsteps for a year-round Hallowe'en, and you can't buy them off with pound coins or home-baked biscuits. They have no use for money and they only eat meat.

Good people of England, we interrupt your weekend break at the theme park to bring you an exclusive report: all your forgotten children are waking up early from their unmarked graves. Somebody forgot to tell them they need to take responsibility for their own lives, and now they're pointing their fingers and shouting with fierce voices.

Good people of England, lock your doors and keep all the lights on, your untold dead are rising.

RAY WILLMOTT

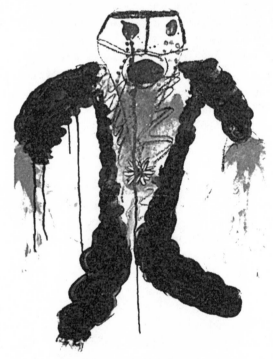

TOP: DEBBIE SUMMERS, AGE SIX
BOTTOM: SELF-PORTRAIT BY DEBBIE SUMMERS
OF HERSELF AT THE AGE OF SIX,
PAINTED DURING THERAPY

## "A stranger" (within)

When we see a strange child crying do we ask why, or do we assume that the child has been told off for being bad, or having a tantrum, and we walk on by? I used to cry. But nobody asked why, so I stopped crying, but the abuse did not stop. Now I am learning to cry again, and to tell of the terrible secret tearing away at my heart.

STEPHEN H. HORTON

## Envoi

Were I to try to write
the story of all child abuse,
my book would go on for ever
like some latter-day Arabian Night story.

Each assaulted child;
those who are grown,
those who are enduring
and those whose suffering is to come,
inhabits with me
a tortured world.

You who can't tell or cry,
whose telling is punished
or not believed
or seen as an excuse for further abuse,
my words are yours.
You are welcome to hold them.

You who can't even tell.
Let the child within me,
who was terrified into silence,

reach out and share your torture
until your own words come
and you can find a kind of safety.

Let your cries and mine together
no longer be ignored
by the deaf parental world,
smug in its self-satisfied complacency,
offering up its children as a sacrifice
because it has forgotten
its own childhood.

Let us create, somehow,
out of the madness that haunts us all,
perpetrators and abused,
a world safe for children,
free from the pollution of violence.

And let's not take forever.

BRENDA NICKLINSON

## An unsolved mystery

SCHOOL WAS FULL OF ITS WONDROUS IDEALS:
HOW WHAT NOT TO DO AND HOW GOOD THAT
    FEELS;
HOW TO LOVE YOUR NEIGHBOR IN FAMINE OR
    FEAST;
HOW TO OBEY YOUR TEACHER, YOUR DOCTOR,
    YOUR PRIEST.

BUT I'VE YET TO SOLVE ONE GREAT MYSTERY:
WHAT TO DO WHEN MY MAMA AND PAPA
    SCREW ME.

RICHIE B.

## Men in control

As an adult survivor of childhood sexual abuse I am very interested in the ways in which we attempt to control each other and allow ourselves to be controlled. Dealing with the aftermath of the abuse has caused me to consider my own feelings of personal power and help-lessness. In reflection, I am also struck by the fact that many of the ways in which survivors were controlled as children can be seen as an extension of the ways in which the more powerful elements in society control the less powerful.

The language of the Christian Church is suffused with the authority of the Lord. Only upon capitulation to that authority will you be blessed. Obedience is a prerequisite for receipt of the tokens of love, as it is in so many families. The government has the sanction of force and violence (the Army and police in situations of industrial unrest for example) and uses the language of Law and Order to justify its actions. Parents sanction the use of their strength, or even violence, against children in order to exercise control. All this contains the implicit messages that it is correct to control (through intimidation, coercion or manipulation) those who are weaker than oneself and that it is either unsafe or wicked to resist openly when subjected to such control.

A natural capacity for empathy, the need to receive and give love and the need to be secure, are warped into control drives—control yourself so that they can't get to you or control them so that you are safe. Control and obedience are implanted from birth. Their effects are sufficiently pervasive that they may even be regarded as part of a natural order.

Social institutions, be they families, self-help groups, schools or political parties, reflect the unrecognized damage of those who create and maintain them. From what other source comes the deadly hypocrisy of governments who serve the interests of their own power base by propaganda, sabotage and warfare? What has created the mind-set of corporate men who disown any responsibility for the welfare of people or planet?

Where can a man say "I have been hurt, can you help me"? How can he be empowered to recognize it when everything points him to close up and deny it? Why should a man relinquish power, relinquish control over others when he (probably unknowingly) perceives that as putting himself at risk? Is it not clear that these individual questions affect the whole of society?

STEVE WILLIAMS

## O! Social Services

Who are we?
We're just numbers with files
Numbers with names
But you don't know us
Why should you?
Some say they care about us kids in care
But still bury their heads
Bad press attitudes just don't help
I can't make much difference
Cos the system stitches us up
We're the most vulnerable group of kids
In that we rely on strangers
To guide us, teach us, help us
And some have been known to abuse us
Take advantage of our circumstances
If we kick up a fuss
There won't be much done
Even if the Bryn Estyn Line is up and running
God bless those who really try to help us
Those who really care
No wonder we want to turn to drugs
Just for a buzz—we tell you
But maybe it's really to escape
Because sometimes it feels like the only escape
Escape—what a strong word, strong need
Do Clwyd really care about us

When a majority of us are left out?
On things like NAYPIC and their AGMs
We should be given the chance to speak out
For what we feel is right and wrong or whatever
These wonder people (NAYPIC) give us the voice
but unfortunately we still rely on you to pass on such info
To tell us when the next meeting is
Allowing us to go—to be heard
We have no real choice—you're the bosses.
We could always rebel but then we're dubbed as
        troublemakers
And not young people who've our opinions and feelings
        about *our* lives
The lives that you adults control
That adults control
Or if you happen to be an adult not long left the so-called
        "care system"
You're not told of such events unless you're very lucky
Surely if Social Services and everybody else are so concerned
about us kids in care they'd make the effort to keep us in the
        know
Even if we're no longer in care—
We're still willing to offer suggestions and help if we can
count us in—we might do some good
After all we've had the first-hand experience
*Have you?*
So go on—PROVE YOU REALLY DO GIVE A DAMN! IF
        YOU CAN!

"CARLA"

---

When we say we were abused by women
We get some funny looks
We're told this is just a fantasy
Cause it's not in our training books.

Women don't abuse, it's just not so,
It's all in your head and you must let it go,
Why won't they believe us, we know the facts,
We are still reliving their unspeakable acts.

TERRI MCLAUGHLIN

## Going to the authorities

I knew that I had to go through with reporting my father, but oh, the pain, the pain was killing me inside and battering my poor heart was so bad, so much. But I had to do it, all the time I knew I had to, for me, for Little Sue, for Isabelle and for everything I believed in.

After the cup of tea I calmed down, and told Brian I was ready to go now to the police station to report my dad for child abuse. And still the tears came down and I couldn't stop them.

When we arrived at the station, as I walked up the steps I turned and looked at the sky and inside my head I said "Can you see me, Dad? Do you know what I am going to do to you?" and Little Elise cried for hurting her daddy, her poor sick daddy who didn't know it was wrong to screw little girls or mess about with their private parts, she cried because she still loved her daddy.

Then I turned and walked in after Brian. And I felt so bad, so unhappy: this was what I had to do but it was killing me inside with pain and hurt.

I was twenty-four years old. And I was reporting my father for child abuse against me.

In the middle of a crowded police waiting room, where everybody could hear, I stood at the desk and the police-lady asked me if she could help. It was all I could do to look at her. And I said: "I want to report my father for child sexual abuse," and she asked who had been abused and I said "Me."

Little Sue, me, I had been abused by my father, so someone please help me to help stop him hurting all the other little girls he came into contact with through his job, and used his money to buy them.

And she told me that someone would be right down to see me. A CID officer came down, a lady, and she took Brian and I up to her office, and we sat while she asked questions and filled in a form, asking for a photo of my father then apologized about having to have done so there in the office and asked if we could arrange a date when I could give a statement, in a comfortable private flat where there would be a kettle or food and could take all day, and I could bring Brian.

And we made a date and time.

And nobody could see my pain.

---

The reasons the officer gave for the case being dropped were these:

The case was too old;

There was not enough evidence—my sister's doctor who had examined her had recorded her bleeding as something that sometimes happens—and my mother had explained it as her shoving a toothbrush up herself;

My sister's refusal to appear in court, even though she had given a statement.

I wrote these down, trying so hard to keep my red red rage from bubbling up, which it was threatening to do.

Perhaps, then, there was still a hope: perhaps my dad's name would go down on the Social Services register then? Perhaps they would be warned what sort of a man he was?

No, the officer explained, my father had not been convicted therefore the Social services were not informed. There was nothing I could do.

What a waste of time, effort and money, and what a lot of pain. And the fury came out. So, my father could go out and do it to other little girls then; he was free to go out and do it again. And the officer said the CID wished they could do more, that there were many men like my father out there that they were powerless to stop. Great.

The only way my father would be convicted was if some other little girl came forward and told the police about him; they would keep his record on file and if any further cases of child abuse came up they would check him out with the other similar cases.

If the little girl had the courage to tell on him, after he had bought her with sweets and taken her out on nice days and poisoned her against the police, *if* the little girl had the courage to go against my father, before the case got too old and *if* she had medical or otherwise evidence.

And *if* she had the courage to go through what I had been through, which had taken me twenty-four years and several years of counselling in one form or another.

There were many ifs and there was only one me. I knew the chances of a little girl, similar to Little Elise, coming forward against all these odds were not even worth writing down.

I began to have a very painful period of counselling. I just don't know how I managed to function. I spent many hours thinking of how I let my sister down, how I had let Little Elise down. Just thinking, wishing I had never started anything, never got my sister's hopes up, never put my family through all the humiliation, just wish I had shut the fuck up and listened to my mother who had told me to let it lie, to leave it be. Cursing my stupid self for wasting my time going to the police when there could have been another, more personal way.

Then, then after many months, I began to think. Very slowly it dawned on me, through all my pain and anguish, that I had not finished. That there was more I could do. That maybe there was hope that my father was feeling bad, that at least my mother and father were divorced and my sisters had the option of seeing him or not. That my mother, who still kept in touch with my father, said that he felt as if he had lost the one daughter he had doted on.

There was still hope, and that hope is to tell the world about people like my father, to open people's eyes through this book.

There is no law in this country that says a man cannot lay his daughter on his stomach, place his penis between—but not inside her tiny vagina—her legs, get her to read stories to his penis, encourage her to cut out pictures of naked women, get her to take photos of him in the nude and ask her to be like a girlfriend to him, and then admit all the above on a signed statement to the police. There is no law that will prosecute a man who admits all the above, or else I would have damn well had that court case and won. All the evidence, from my sisters, my friends, the statements from my counselors, all wasted because the law

is an ass and lets perverts like my father roam the streets after everything I have done, after the pain and the agony I have lived through.

ANONYMOUS

## A witness

You want a witness?
for what he did?
Those hands that held me
in the night,
and that body that crushed
my very limbs.

A witness?
For everything's ok I won't
hurt you.
Everyone knows we do this and
it's ok

A witness?
For you may be twelve, but in bed
you're twenty-one.

A witness?
For him sneaking through to my
room at night when everyone
slept.

A witness?
For the pain inside me, and I
would grip at the pillow
so very tight.

A witness?
For my head being held.

My mouth being forced to do things
which made me feel sick.

A witness?
For the tears I cried when someone
asked me what was wrong, and I'd
open my mouth and the words wouldn't
come.

A witness?
For the screams that wouldn't come.

YOU WANT A WITNESS . . .

ALICE LIDDELL


## Care in the nineties

PEDOPHILES PASS THE WAD,
GUILT GRIPS THE WHORE,
POLITICIANS LEGISLATE,
FOR "MORE, MORE, MORE."

RICHIE B.


## Dear Mum and Dad

I'm writing to say I'm sorry, I've made a terrible mistake. I've just heard there's a proper medical name for what I've done: false memory syndrome. How clever you were to have known about it all along! While I was thinking I'd discovered a horrific truth about our family, you knew that I had no evidence that would stand up in court, and that therefore I was lying. Because, of course, you were the adults at the time, and I a pre-school child, you would *know* what you had or had not done. *Your* memories would be clear and objective, whereas the mind of a child—well, we all know what sorts of things little children fantasize about!

So, as you suggested in your letter, Dad, I must be ill to even dream such a thing about my own father. Well at least this new syndrome represents some medical progress. Let's hope they've got it right this time. I quite prefer the label to the old ones—endogenous depression, manic depression, personality disorder. I suppose those earlier experts just didn't have enough information, before the false memory research, to work out what was really going on.

*You* hadn't worked it out then either, had you, telling people I'd had a breakdown because I couldn't cope with the competition at university. Even for *me* three suicide attempts, a course of ECT and twenty-eight days in the locked ward of a mental hospital were a bit OTT for a fit of intellectual pique.

So I am grateful to the discoverers of this new syndrome for clearing up all the confusion. Fancy me, after all that mental illness, thinking I might know better than you what was real! (Don't worry, if you didn't cause the mental illness by abusing me, I'm not going to blame it on your bad parenting instead—the doctors at the hospital always said it was biological.)

You're quite right, as well, about these feminist therapists trying to undermine the family. No, they weren't all lesbians: four of the five I've talked to about my "memories" were heterosexual, two of them mothers—but doesn't that just go to show how far this conspiracy has spread?

I don't think *they* manipulated *me* though, it was more the other way round. They were so easily duped! All I did was describe my childhood—you know, all those wet knickers and nightmares, being sexually aware at five, attempting intercourse with five little boys when I was ten, I presume you did know about all that? How I tried to damage penises with kicks and sticks in the school playground? And believing I was really a boy, you remember those boys" clothes you used to dress me in, Mum? (But perhaps I never told you how frightened I was of Dad, and how his body revolted me. You see, I thought that was normal.) Then I told them how terrified I was when my breasts and periods started, and how all through secondary school I was afraid someone would find out I wasn't like all the other girls.

Then I described my adult difficulties with men, the desperate promiscuity to hide my terror of penetration, the sexual entanglements with friends' fathers and male authority figures, the suicidal depressions, the self-mutilation, the belief that as a child I had committed an unforgivable crime—and they believed me! When I told them I suspected I'd been abused, they actually said that it seemed quite likely. They didn't even mention that I might be mentally ill or making it all up! You see how easily it was done, just by trotting out a few details.

Only one therapist suggested I might be mistaken, funnily enough the only man I consulted. He said that sexual abuse within families was rare, and emotional insecurity more damaging to a child than a bit of inappropriate fondling. If only I'd listened to him! He did offer to hypnotize me to uncover the truth, but naturally I did not take up this opportunity.

So let me tell you how these therapists encouraged me to believe my father was a rapist. First they let me do lots of talking, and just listened, so that I started to believe I had something important to say. Then they got me feeling *all sorts of emotions I didn't have before* like grief and rage. I mean, who would feel like that unless someone planted it in them?

I kept having these episodes that were like reliving being raped, orally raped. But I couldn't see anything, only *feel* it. Well, you're right, what sort of a memory is that? I can't even say exactly what age I was! And of course, Mum, if this had really happened when I was only three or four I would have been able to tell you everything. And obviously if Dad denies it why shouldn't you believe him? Yes, I did tell the therapists that you were both professional people and very respectable but I don't think they took that into account. They're very clever. In the end, they said that I had to make up my own mind about what happened—subtle, isn't it?

*They* didn't tell me to stop seeing you; that was my own decision, as much as I'm capable of making one. I just thought life would be easier without a family, you know, not having to bother with cards on Mother's Day or having to visit anyone at Christmas. All that cry-

ing over soap operas, wanting to belong to someone, feeling be-
reaved—well that just showed I was really missing you. You know
how I've always liked to be different! Like not having any sort of career or financial security. I've been quite comfortable, really, living
on benefit, going out every week to therapy, blaming everything on
you. For a while there, I even thought my life made some kind of
sense, that I'd found an *explanation* but of course you don't get that
with a mental illness, do you?

Thank God I've got parents who want me so much they're prepared to forgive me, even welcome me back into the family as long
as I withdraw my accusation and admit that I'm mentally ill. I'm so
grateful that you want me that badly. Since I stopped seeing you six
years ago, you have each written me one letter, describing how I have
ruined your retirement. Of course, if you hadn't mentioned it, I would
never have stopped to think about the effect on you, never felt a
twinge of guilt. You must be right about me always being selfish, as
well as a clever liar.

There's just one thing that confuses me—nobody else seems to
think I'm mentally ill, and my friends tell me I'm a decent, honest
sort of person. Do you think they're humoring me? After all, it takes
your own loving parents to really know you, and to have the courage
to tell you the truth.

I remain your daughter, as always . . .

RUNA WOLF

## Living in a daydream
### (FMS—the nineties nightmare)

Celebrate, that's what they told me
Life's a celebration
Looks like I'm
Bang up against a gable-end

So, come and tear me apart
Why don't you

Chop up the parts
That give you such sore eyes?

Here's a bleeding heart
Quick, throw it in the bin
While no one else is looking
Wouldn't want them to see

VD made me barren
So, let's destroy my womb
Eczema scarred my feet for life
A good excuse to stop me walking

I am a hypochondriac
False Memory Syndrome
Pluck out my eyes
So I no longer cry

My tiny, pathetic hopes
For some kind of empathy
Boomerang
Slice my tongue apart

Oh, put a gag in your mouth
They say
Your words sordid, rotten crimes
Why didn't you take your soma?

Must have been
Alcohol in my blood surrogate
I reply
What else explains this madness?

They say they're on my side
I will be their Beauty Queen
Triumph over Tragedy, *Woman's Own* style
Amelia Earhart's come back to life

I will be pretty as you please
I am your cute little thing
I will dance and sing
flutter my eyelashes, so delicate and vulnerable

Burn my cheap diaries
Exorcise my dreams
No, I've never been hurt
I'm just sick in my head

So sweet the anesthetic
My head is light
Lobotomized
Lady in White

Celebrate the myth
Salve your conscience
Sleep well tonight, my sisters

KOURTNEY TEMYATIN


## Middle-class girls

I'm no blond haired, blue-eyed, middle-class southern bride
Bumming round with the proles till it's time to go home
To Surrey.

I've got no glittering career, contacts made by Daddy dear
No management hand on my rear
Can stuff that.
And I'm not here slumming it
On some lukewarm existential trip
I'm getting a life in this unemployment blip
You hear me?

Not scared of muggers on the stairs
Not freaked out by their wide-eyed glares
Wasn't them robbed me, left a hole I can't repair
Eh Daddy?

No, cos
Middle-class girls don't feel no pain
Middle-class girls don't ever complain
Middle-class girls don't go mad

Middle-class girls don't show they're sad
Middle-class girls clench their teeth
Numb those feelings out of reach.

Well, this middle-class girl's provoking
This middle-class girl's evoking
Memories of a childhood choking
And I won't swallow any more
Daddy.

ANONYMOUS


## Childline

I feel so alone
I feel nobody can help
Friends just don't want to listen
But they don't know how I felt
Their home life is different from mine
Their family really care
They never have to wonder if their family will always be
    there
It's been four years now that I've endured all this pain
And just when I think it's over
It starts all over again

Mum has been drinking
She's in a world of her own
She doesn't realize I need her
I need my home
Dad can't cope under all the strain
It's gone to his head, sometimes I wish I were dead
It seems to be my fault
The way that they act
But it's not, I know that for a fact
But that doesn't stop them hitting me
From blaming me for their wrongs
I can't remember a happy home life
Has it really been this long
I'm so scared I don't know what to do
Isn't there anyone that can help me see this through
Then my friend told me there's someone that can help on the
       line
So I rang and you listened
You helped me see it through
Thanks seems such a meaningless word
But I'd like to say it to you
Things might not have changed much at home
In fact they're still the same
But now I can cope with it better
Myself I no longer blame
So thank you Childline for being there
For helping me see it through
And to all the children you've helped in the world
We would like to say thank you.

ANN WILLBOURNE

# Can you hear?

Does anyone hear?
Or, even listen?
To my cries for help.

Too polite to say exactly
You know . . . ?
It's a guessing game.

Have you heard?
Did you only listen?
What sound reached your ear?
Was it a joke
    A passing unimportant utterance
    A fleeting comment
    A superfluous sentence part
    of regular conversation.
I screamed
I cried
I begged for help

But I was too afraid to be explicit
You had to guess
You had to listen
and you had to hear.

But no one heard
In silence I howled
In loneliness I sat with friends
In confusion I clearly saw
I laughed sadly
I am surrounded by a deaf crowd.

A. IYATO BAMGBOSE

# Telling it as it is

Would you the pain If I am
listen is constant I sick
if I that it told of
really interferes you surviving
told that it I Now
you destroys was I
what concentration afraid will
it's Or of tell
like would sleep you
Could you of the
you say my terror
cope I body the
if I can't Or sickness
said hear would are
there is the you always
no pain say with
happy Tell I me
endings me can't I
Only death about You just
Would you your are hide
listen strength a it
if I Would survivor because
said you Listen others
listen now want
happy
endings

REBECCA MOTT

## Where are the medals for us?

Where are the medals for us?
For walking here,
On our own two feet
Where are the lover's arms,
Welcoming home?
Where are the warm beds,
To rest our tired feet?
Where are the friends to finish our work?

Where are the ticker-tape parades,
For the lonely heroes?
Where the prizes,
For the tests we ran?
Where are the welcoming gloves and warm hands,
To hold us up as we fail the last?

Nowhere. I can see
So we just keep walking,
For there are no medals for us.

AIRB

## Knowing a darkness

Knowing a darkness
Evil is never believed in any language

Pain too real somehow hits our primordial past
Becoming myth and legend

And no one will bear witness to our truth
Empty and silent
No museum will be made

As memorial to our suffering
And it goes on
Screamed in the papers
Another fashion sensation

Who really believes enough to
Fight indifference or challenge denial?

It's too hard to be alone with truth
It's too hard to cry for the children of the world
Adults are children divorced from their past
Running so fast to create a future to hide in
Making babies in order to forget, living out fears
Which wreak their own suffering

Let us not hide from our shadows
Feeding them on silence and secrecy
As they grow too monstrous to see
Too hungry to restrain

And the crimes of stealth and cunning continue unnoticed
In clean white houses with neatly clipped lawns
At night, memories are blanked, bodies disconnected as
They are ravaged in search of feelings denied
Souls leave when the pain is too hard to bear
Wild roses thrown out with the rubbish
Minds cannot comprehend love in conjunction with hate
We cannot understand why those we depend on to survive
Should want us to die, fearing or wishing ourselves dead
And torture is not recognized in suburbia
And sadism is not talked about in Surrey
And rape is not real in Richmond
And no one will believe in ritual abuse

Shall we hide our visions of burning bodies
Shall we interpret feelings of strangulation

Shall we dismiss memories of gang rape, humiliation,
Blood and sperm as fantasy?

They knew no one would believe their crimes
They count on a society which refuses to recognize itself
Where we divide ourselves to bear the pain
And sacrifice knowledge for cold comfort

When will I know
When will I know that you know
When will I rejoice that the world knows itself
When will we act to end the suffering?

---

Treatment is for Perpetrators
Victims need Healing

CHARIS ALLAND

## A case for Amnesty International

I'm finding it difficult
to get your attention,
to tell you what it's like.
So, as one adult to another
here are the facts.

A person is imprisoned,
not told the charges
or the length of sentence.
Every week
one man takes the person
by the hand to a group of men
waiting in a deserted room.

The men strip and torture
the person with a knife,
and repeatedly rape
all the body's openings.
The person is then taken back
and put to bed and threatened
not to tell.

Usually this would be a case for
Amnesty International or even the police.
But the person is a three-year-old child,
one of the men her father,
the house is down the street from her home.

This prison is not seen.
It goes unrecognized,
until the child, grown,
attempts to speak.

WENDY COLYER

## Political survival

Surviving is a political and revolutionary act. I believe we are on the
verge of revolution more sweeping than any which has preceded it.
It is profound because it is grounded in the personal experience of
many thousands of survivors. It has no leader, no formal structure and
no need of arms manufacture, but it may take centuries to complete.

To experience the reality of abuse and come out the other
side, whole and informed, gives us a keenness of perception for the
corruption of human spirit upon which too much of society is
founded. Society cannot both acknowledge that experience and
remain unchanged. How, for example, would a sergeant major behave if he were in touch with the vulnerability of his inner child?
Would a U.S. president behave differently if he or she had been enabled to work through a traumatic childhood? The entrenched de-

nial in our societies makes these questions, for the moment, slightly ludicrous.

I believe that it is not possible for someone who has worked through the pain of their own abuse to continually act it out nor to knowingly and deliberately harm fellow life forms. But for me the point of key significance about the preceding sentence is that it can be written and understood. It contains implicitly the use of ideas such as Denial and the True Self. Never before have such expressions of psychological reality been in the public domain.

Never before have we had the language and frames of reference with which to bring issues surrounding child sexual abuse and its effects into public society. This is now available to us and is still being developed by therapists and survivors alike.

There are now too many of us who understand our experience to be silenced, and the core of therapeutic knowledge is too well established to be subverted. But we only have to witness the strident antics of the False Memory Syndrome Foundation (who would more properly be named the Pedophile Supporters Club) to see a foreshadow of the reaction against the progress of truth.

How will the voice of the True Self be heard by the forces of denial and control? The controlling interests behind the status quo have much to lose, but what illusions are they trying to protect?

Every step forward each survivor takes puts another stone in the bedrock of this revolution, even though this may be far from our minds when we are struggling with our personal histories. We are just beginning to fight back and we are many. Who knows where revolution will lead?

STEVE WILLIAMS

# Us!

We decided to end the anthology with a collection of pieces and statements about *us*. We hope that you will agree that this chapter speaks for itself and needs no further introduction.

The day must come when men, regardless of their sexual preferences, will be given the same levels of consideration and understanding that courageous women are now forcing through. It is often said that women are allowed to be victims, whereas men are always the aggressors. Well I can vouch for that in my particular case, but I would prefer to see that stereotypical myth destroyed and it be accepted that both men and women can be abusers, and that both men and women can be victims. I dream of the day when I can with pride, and without fear, say, "YES, I AM A SURVIVOR!" and this not be met with an embarrassed silence or an exaggerated display of concern that treats me like an emotional cripple.

I neither ask for, nor deserve, your pity: I am too busy enjoying my new-found life to waste time on that. Pity serves no purpose other than to debilitate, whereas rage can be a powerful catalyst if channeled in the right way. It is my rage that has turned me from being a *victim* of abuse into a living breathing *survivor*.

PAUL

## Woman of granite

If I close my eyes
I see the way
Undisturbed by daylight
Free from the distortions
Of daily living,
Offering a vibrant alternative
To living death.

And yet my girlhood
Has imbued me
With the art of self-denial:
To be not only deaf
But also dumb and blind
To my own human needs:
For I am woman.

Rise, woman of granite,
Stand firm and proud
In your humanity;
Articulate your inner self,
Let go the straight-lacing
Around your living body
And go free!

Stretch out your limbs,
Release your bonds,
Open wide your eyes
To the horizon of possibility,
Reach out your hand
And allow your sensate palm
To touch life.

CARO

## Do you speak Barbarian?

I feel the need to say something about the way I have used, in my poetry, the cannibal image. Not so much to explain its meaning—I hope the poems do that—but to describe how important the image is to me, how it has helped to give me a positive view of my whole self.

In the early days of dealing with the recovery of memories of sexual abuse, the term "survivor" seemed enough. I've always preferred it to "victim," and at first it seemed an adequate description of what I was doing—keeping my head above water (just) despite being far out in a treacherous sea. More recently, "surviving" seems too passive a word to describe my response to the abuse. It does hint at the possibility of witnessing for those who did not make it, of being able to give an eyewitness account. But sexual abuse is not like an air disaster. It is, horrifically, about a relationship.

Although passivity may be the best defense for a child or teenager abused by a powerful adult, the inner strategies used to survive are active and creative. They may turn out to be "unhealthy" and life-limiting when the danger has literally passed. But to define them only in terms of textbook neuroses or defense mechanisms misses the point. I'm sick of both medical labels and the active terminology applied to the abuser's deeds—rape, molestation, violation, assault, pederasty, pedophilia—all of which turn me into an object. How many words do we have to describe our experience *actively*? I don't mean to imply that victims of abuse are actively involved in the abusing. I'm not talking about collusion or seduction. (I dislike the word incest because for me it implies something shared.) Victims do *not* share the responsibility for their abuse. But the words we have, the doing words, are all labels for what the abuser does. If we have survived, we have not just been passive. On some level, to exist at all involves fighting back.

I wanted a word that captured my will to live, my courage and endurance, a word that made more of the fighting spirit of survival. A word that named my side of the experience so that I was neither a completely passive victim, simply "done to," or a neurosis-riddled casualty. Calling myself a cannibal instead of a victim of oral abuse makes me feel powerful, angry, brave, and very proud. In the context of my poems, the cannibalistic deed *I* performed was an act of courage. It was a desperate, shocking act, unspeakable and unthinkable for me for many years—yet it was the act that saved my life. I made a life-saving *choice*. I *did* it. I was hungry for love, and this was the only "nourishment," laced with hatred, that my father gave me. On his part, this was disgusting, unforgivable. On my part, it was a choice between do or die. Could a child have been braver than this? What an affirmation of my will to live!

I started working towards this definition of myself in "A recipe for wholemeal bread." I had been haunted by food imagery, struggling to find a way to digest the indigestible. I wanted to transform, by my own creativity, my own body (which includes the experience of having sex forced down my throat) into something truly nourishing, from which I could draw strength. I needed to feed myself the love, acceptance and nurturing I had been deprived of, but also to "swallow" the awful truth about my past. In this poem, it is a struggle to distinguish myself from the abuse, to separate my body from the abuser's. The white-hot oven is the rage I know I need to complete the process, to remake—rebake—my own body so that I can fully inhabit it, and enjoy it, again. The triumph at the end of this poem is more optimistic than real. I knew, then, that the fullness of my talents, my ability to feel satisfaction, the self-esteem my childhood had robbed me of, had all been buried along with the memories of abuse. I knew that only by re-owning the abused part of myself, somehow fully digesting—*reincorporating*—the abuse and all its implications, would I ever grow to my full height and strength.

In "Cannibal Docks article one" the character Cannibal begins to explore her powers. She is still part of me, but is expanding to embody the active spirit of survival, the rage of the abused—she is becoming a sort of avenging angel. She is always compassionate, never forgetting the horrors of her past. She still speaks as and for the abused child. But she has also all the power of an enraged adult, all the perceptiveness of one who has no illusions to lose. In this poem she takes on the patriarchal idea of truth and justice, embodied in the law court, where "the man in wig and frock" is unable to see or hear the reality of the abused child because he is only interested in "hard evidence" and external "facts." Cannibal exposes the penis as the "measuring stick" against which much of our female reality is compared and found to be—invisible. The terminology surrounding questions of truth, in a legal sense, is laden with masculine sexual imagery, the *stiff* questioning which leads to the *hard* evidence *standing up* in court. In comparison with men's own visible, external sexual anatomy, female sexuality is interior, hidden from public view, and therefore suspect? Men, it seems, do not like to have to rely on "our word."

"My word" for what happened to me, my experience of abuse, would not be adequate in a law court. It has not been enough for most of my family. And anyway, what are "our words" for being abused? It seems we have none that truly describe our experiences unless we invent them for ourselves. To the extent that we are forced to communicate in a language that is not our own, that does not name our experiences, *all* women are orally abused. Cannibal champions the right of all those denied access to the power of naming (all whose speech is queer) to define reality for themselves. She is a prodigy in her native tongue, a true Barbarian—a "civilized" word for the "stuttering" of foreigners—celebrating her own lore and language for those who are not afraid to see, and listen.

Historically, "cannibal" is a white man's term, used to create a moral separation between "civilization" and the "primitive" peoples native to some of the lands white colonists wished to appropriate. Cannibal, as a survivor of sexual abuse, knows the secret truth about that "civilization." She also inhabits a land colonized and named by an invader, a land peopled with all the projected qualities the masculine psyche refuses to own. She turns the hypocrisy of the "upright" male back upon him, confronting him with his own vice. Cannibal, in the sense of the word which I have given it, is the first word in my own language. Cannibal is, on all levels, about speaking out, about answering—and biting—back. Naming myself a cannibal is the start of inhabiting a world peopled with my own meanings and values. It gives me energy, space to move around in, and it's fun!

RUNA WOLF

## A recipe for wholemeal bread
## (for a malnourished girl-child)

First take some grits of dried-up hope,
an ounce will do. Bathe in tears
and sweeten with a memory of the womb.
Keep warm for many years, nestled in an armpit
or between the thighs, until the surface froths,
a dizzying head of beer breath,
cellar-dank, mold of leather, vinegar-sour.

Now give body to your desire,
an armful, or two, of coarse-ground flour,
a pinch of Lot's wife's sin,
a palmful of oil to slide the fingers in.
Squeeze and rub and meld until
the dough takes form, an amputated limb,
goose-pricked, clammy, pale.

You must take courage now and roll
this yielding flesh between your fists
until the hidden gut within resists,
springs firm, and dimpled with a smile.

Now cradle in an ample lap, your own is best,
until your bread-child rises like a buttock
or the moon, replete
with giddy mis-conception's fizz.
This part is hard, your heel of hand must beat
the bloated belly, force its phantoms out
to face the sobering air. Knead it now,
with vigor, and you'll feel the tug
of unrequited hunger suck
your fingers clean.

Bake in a white-hot oven, do not flinch,
let fire transmute your golem 'til it speaks
of malted oysters, seaweed,
sun-licked skin. And when the hollow knock
invites you in, allow to cool: remember, it is he who breaks
who makes the crust and under-table crumb.
This is your body, daughter, whole, no longer dumb,
lean with long-fermented lust, robust with greed.
Take it, name it, eat it all.

RUNA WOLF

---

have you heard how they wandered?
those night-things-night-like owl-like they wandered
for years and called piteous and mewing like sea birds
        strangled.
have you heard what became of them?
at the end of many years they looked at each other
and said
stuff this for a lark
and threw off their night-likenesses and began to laugh
and live with their boots on
and happily ever after
or so I was told

LIZZY COTTRELL

## Nadia

In a time not too far away from this one, lived a small girl. Her name
was Nadia, and she lived with her family and many cats in an old
wooden house surrounded by countryside. Nadia liked to wander in

nature alongside animals and trees, she was very happy with her life and what it offered her.

Then one day her brother began to lay his hands upon her small body. They were very heavy and cruel, the weight of them almost crushed her to death. She went to her parents and tried to tell them of the dark monster that had entered her sanctuary. But no matter how loud she screamed, they could not hear. Their ears fell deaf from that day forward and they no longer listened to a word she said.

Nadia felt very alone. She was so greatly affected by this whole experience that it struck her like a blow to the head, knocking her spirit clean out of her eye sockets. Her spirit was in such a hurry to leave this frightful situation that it fled without telling her how to live. Nadia did not know how to breathe life in and breathe life out. So she carried on living but only breathed in and breathed in and never let any out.

She began to swell with each breath of air. Her brother soon left her alone. Nadia went on like this for years. At first she could almost live life normally but soon she grew so big that she could no longer walk. And not too long after that she could not even fit inside the house. There was nothing else she could do so she just lay down in the dirt, day and night, as still as a huge old rock.

People soon began to notice this and they came to look at her. When they stared into her eyes they could see the emptiness of the Universe. This sight was very disturbing and sent many people, even the strongest and the most brave, scrambling for their lives. Nadia's cats, however, kept her company, prowling around her quiet form and guarding her from further danger. They licked the sweat from her skin on hot days and snuggled into her rising belly on cold nights to keep her warm.

While this was going on Nadia's spirit wandered all over the place, neither happy nor sad, just scared. She was quite tired but always too afraid to stop for very long, especially in the dark of night.

She burrowed into the Earth Mother and lived amongst worms and grubs feeding on the dead and soaking in the warmth and moisture from the soil. But this did not console her. She travelled down many streams and rivers, splashing with fish, chasing turtles or just simply becoming one with the spirit of the water and floating and tumbling with its life force. But no one could offer her advice. She swayed with the grass in the open plains. She hunted with wild dogs, tearing carcasses to pieces with her teeth and claws but still she did not shake her fear. She crashed with the waves of the salted seas, pounding rocks and sand until she was tattered and tired. She raced with dolphins and sang with whales but nothing comforted her being. She ran with the wind and whispered with the breezes, chasing birds and whipping people's faces with dust but nothing could settle these feelings.

On the darkest, coldest nights, when the moon hid behind woolly clouds she would snuggle into a fire hugging coals to her chest and stomach, in the hope of burning off her horrible pain. Nothing seemed to work.

One day she decided to travel to the sun because she thought if she could get close enough she would never have to endure the heaviness of evening again. She went to her friend the wind and asked if it could help carry her, at least part of the way, because she had lost much of her strength on the journey trekked so far. The wind agreed, so she climbed upon its back and flew at a great speed.

When she reached the sun a wise red woman awaited her. The woman took the tired soul in her arms and nurtured her with molten honey. Nadia's spirit was worn and frayed and covered in thorns, but with the help of the wise red woman's care and knowledge of all things, she became healthy and strong.

With time, the wise red woman drove the fear from her heart and with much love sent her back from where she had come. Nadia's spirit returned with haste; there was not much time left. She found an older girl's body lying on the damp earth, who was absolutely huge. She looked into her face and almost didn't recognize her.

The spirit entered the body through the nose as it took yet another breath in. Nadia's body began to glow and tingle. She slowly began to breathe out. Her breath became a warm breeze which swept over the land, spreading pollen and seeds, helping birds to fly and warming the winter chill from all around. She stood up slowly feeling quite happy with herself. She rubbed her eyes and looked around at everything.

## About myself

"I am a survivor, I am a survivor, I am a survivor." I repeat this to my-self with my eyes closed so that I will remember, I remembered, I will always remember.

I am following the trail back to myself. Trying to tie myself back together so I can understand my life as a whole person. As a child my feelings were numbed, I was broken into pieces. Now I have learned to be true to myself. I have also learned that it is important to trust yourself and to find others who can be trusted. I do not have to live my life alone, I have already lived like that. It is also vital to know where you begin and end, to know what is yours and to own that. My space, my life, my body. I do not want to be *only* a survivor, I don't want this pain to consume my whole life and being. I am free to be all that I can. I must be strong for myself alone but understand that I am weak also. Lastly, I know that I am mortal and to heal and to live means to always be learning, no one has all the answers . . . ever. I am a survivor but I am also a sculptor, a drawer, a painter, an active feminist, a fire dancer and a fire breather.

NADIA

*(If I am in the book could you just call me Nadia and not use my last name as I don't like that. My last name represents the loss of identity of all the women in my family before me and the power that men have in my family and society. Thank you.)*

Snuggling into the coals of a fire on the new moon.

NADIA

## Mary's song

(Can be sung to the tune of "Let me Go, Lover")

Letting go,
Letting go,
Letting go—finally
Easing up,
Loosening up
From your spell.
Wiping out
giving back
Heading on—bravely,
Freeing me
Being me
No longer trapped.

*Chorus:*

I like me now
I have fun now
I'm happier—less afraid,
I am a person
In my own right
I'm on parade—
    Not in the shade.

Opening up
Speaking out,
Holding my own—firmly,
Discovering me
Following me
A brand new life.

MARY J. MCMAHON

## My rite of passage

I, Ruth Mary Jackson, am giving myself a new name.

By doing this I am giving myself a gift—a gift of a new beginning, the chance to lay down my own new and healthy roots and to grow and become who I want to be.

I give to Ruth the names of Charis and Alland.

Charis, remembering the Greek Goddess of everything that imparts graciousness to life. The three graces of Aglaia—triumph and splendor; Euphrosyne—cheerfulness; and Thalia—the grace to bloom.

Alland is my gift and acknowledgement of the positive influence and amazing affection Ollie has given to me. Taken from his Great-Grandparents, it symbolizes also an attachment to roots in a family far greater than a biological family—a universal family which enhances life and growth.

By this act I am denying neither my past nor who I am or have been, but affirming my right to be, my right to let go, my right to be liberated. I move away from the names Ruth Mary Jackson to symbolize the movement of my own continuing journey away from the torment and imprisonment which has kept me victim to the past. I let go of those names to make way for something new.

My journey has only started. Today I set a precedent for that journey. It is not an act of magic to create a different person but my Rite of Passage, my Baptism. Most of all it is a Celebration of everything I am and everything I will become.

Today I embrace Charis Ruth Alland as myself and my life.

### I can

I can do many things
Good or evil
In between
With no one to tell me what to do
So what do I do?
Whatever I want
Because: I can

AIRB

### My first year as a known survivor

It is now about a year since I started to remember my childhood sexual abuse. My grandfather buggered me when I was about three years old. He died when I was four. I am still angry about what he did, about suffering its effects for thirty years and nobody noticing, and also because he died and I can't expose him for what he was or confront him with my adult, righteous anger and indignation.

At first I spent about a month in total shock. I had suddenly become a victim of something that happened thirty years ago. It was also a great relief to finally know why I felt so awful deep down inside that I had been having therapy for two years. At least now I knew what I had to deal with. Fortunately, the self-acknowledgement came during a therapy session. Expert and sympathetic help was on hand.

Throughout this year and that initial month I have held down a full-time job as a management accountant. I must have been on automatic pilot that first month, otherwise I just don't know how I'd have done it. I do know I made a large and obvious error at work. This forced me to go to my personnel officer to explain what was happening to me. The remainder of the buried memories and feelings felt like an assassin waiting in the darkness. I needed to disclose the fact that I had post-traumatic stress syndrome to protect myself, my job and to explain the possibility that I might suddenly need to leave a meeting because of triggered memories.

In mid-March I started a one day per fortnight day release course to study for my professional exams. The prospect of being in a crowded tube in London rush hour was very frightening to my suddenly fragile personality. Previously it would only have been one of modern life's irritations, but I have never liked crowded places or small white rooms. Now it seemed daunting and required half a therapy session and planning to overcome. I would imagine sending my inner child to play with some nice toys in a field with the sun shining and some pigs and horses in the next field for company. My therapist taught me this trick. It worked, and I made it. However, I recall looking at a fellow passenger and deciding that he definitely had the face of an abuser. He must have reminded me in some way of my grandfather whose features I cannot recall (and now do not wish to). Hopefully the passenger remained in blissful ignorance of my thoughts.

The homework recommended for the course was 20-30 hours per week. This was further stress, but also an absorbing break from the resurgence of memories and feelings.

At the end of March the dinghy racing season began. I have spent most Sundays this year racing in a two-man dinghy as crew. My club was a place of respite from actively healing, but also healing and recharging in itself: a fun place with lots of camaraderie, a common purpose and people around me who care about me. When you are on the water you only think about one thing—sailing! It certainly blows the cobwebs away. During August I also spent some Saturday afternoons at the club racing on my windsurfer. I felt a little guilty at not being at home studying, but reasoned that I would probably achieve little sitting at my desk, hankering for wind and sunshine. I may not be very good at nurturing my inner child, but at least now she gets plenty of opportunities to play!

Gerry joined the club this summer, in the same class that I race in. We have become firm friends with mutual support as the aim. Gerry supports me and I support him through his divorce and the loss of his children. I never used to have many friends, and certainly no male friends. Remembering has become understanding for me in this respect. Gerry and I also spent Christmas together, mainly fixing my car in his garage. Since then he has helped me to find a new job by giving me a practice interview, printing my c.v. and lending me some useful books. I am currently sewing some bean bags for him. I never thought I could be friends with a man, but now I have several male friends.

Memories have gradually been returning, especially feelings, throughout the year. I remember parts of all the day that the abuse occurred, even the physical pain afterwards, but not the abuse itself. It was a couple of months before I could face the hurt and betrayal of the fact that it was my paternal grandfather who abused me. I had previously felt that I was someone special to him, and in later life I mourned the loss of him. Ironically, I had thought that I would have been better protected from the mental abuse that occurred in my childhood if he had been there to temper it and give me some nurturing. My emotions went up and down like a pendulum, and I wrote a poem about it.

In September I joined a survivors' group set to meet for ten weekly sessions. I had some grave reservations about being in a group and how I would react to the relating of gruesome tales. Fortunately my fears were not played out in reality. However, I did feel very confronted after the first meeting (basically because of the concentration of pain I could feel around me). I went to work for two days, gradually feeling lower and lower, struggling on although every moment was harder. On the third day I phoned work and said I needed some personal time. A day off was agreed. I spent some time huddled under a duvet on my sofa with Sylvester (my cuddly toy) for comfort, and finally managed to cry. Afterwards I felt much better and went back to work the next day. A new group was formed in January and the next day I recognized the same symptoms from my inability to get out of bed. I didn't struggle this time, I just phoned in for a day off. The group understand exactly what I feel because they feel it themselves and no instant cures are expected. I have also made some new friends. We usually go for some pizza, or something, when the group is not formally meeting. The group has been very open, with discussion of some very painful topics, but has also contained a lot of laughter to balance the tears. I wrote a spoof report for the organizers: although it was too esoteric to submit, it was fun writing it.

In November I successfully sat my final exams, although it didn't feel like it at the time. Four exams on day one and day three. Day two is designed for stewing! On day two I had a "feeling small" attack and spent an hour on the phone being coached by my therapist. It did the trick. Thank you.

Yippee! Passed my exams, so now I can look for a new job. Going for interviews really picked me up. Spending time telling someone who is interested in you about all the things you have achieved in your recent career really works on the inside of you, as well as on them. At one interview with Disney Stores there was a three-foot-high Donald Duck next to my chair. Now that's my kind of company! I decided that I wouldn't pursue it further though, as I already had another, much closer offer. Talking to the recruitment agents afterwards, they joked: "Wasn't it nice of them to put Donald there, so you could have a cuddle if you were feeling insecure." I was laughing because they were close to the truth and didn't know it.

About a month ago I heard about this anthology and decided to find out some more. At the weekend I went to the workshop. A room full of survivors looks like a room full of ordinary people. Naturally I zoomed in on the "humor" group in the afternoon. Funnily enough, ours was the noisiest group (laughter—the best medicine, of course).

Disclosure has been a big issue for me throughout this year. I felt strongly about not covering up what was happening to me, or had happened. I needed to explain to my close friends why I felt so fragile and insecure, so I set about telling them that I had started to remember my childhood sexual abuse and a little about why the memories are sometimes repressed. They have all been supportive and caring.

I was forewarned of the difficulties and dangers of disclosure to close family members, so this didn't start until the autumn. By accident I told my sister on the phone one evening. She was upset and angry on my behalf. I went to see her one evening to talk some more. I didn't really feel very much at first, apart from apprehension, but I cried on her shoulder. It was a great comfort to me to be believed. The problems have come since then, mainly because I later remembered my grandmother's part in covering up for my grandfather. My sister has always been my grandmother's favorite, and I felt betrayed when my sister invited her for the weekend to talk to her and assess whether she believed what I felt and knew, or not—all, of course, without revealing the sexual abuse! My sister doesn't believe my grandmother actively connived to cover up for her husband. She raised the issue again at the weekend, and it sounds so rational and convenient *for her*. I *know* my grandmother connived because I remember what she said to my father and I trust my gut feelings in the matter (far more now than I ever did before). The best that I can hope for is that she will change her mind, but failing that, that we can agree to differ. I don't want to lose my sister, but I am not going to deny what my grandmother did or how I feel about her: that would be abusing the child I was all over again. She deserved, and deserves, better.

Telling my mother about two months ago was a big event. I asked her if she would come to stay with me for a weekend so that we could talk about something important. That was before Christmas. I had to allay her fears without telling her what I wanted to discuss. As the time drew near, my worries increased, especially when my mother said she wanted to stay an extra night. I thought she planned to give me a right talking-to about something. It never occurred to me that she just wanted to spend some time with me! The day before her arrival I spent a therapy session preparing to protect myself from the worst possible outcome, but I always believed that she would have believed me as a child, if I had only told her. I hadn't told her because my father didn't believe me when his parents denied it. After the session I spent the evening with Gerry to keep my mind off worrying.

We met the next day and went to my flat for lunch and then sat talking. My stomach was churning after half an hour of trying to say, "I suppose you're wondering what I wanted to talk to you about." I told her that it was a difficult subject and not easy to tell. After telling her some of it she was shocked and said, "I don't believe it" about six times. The first three felt like "I don't believe you" but eventually I managed to hear what she was actually saying. At last I said, "It's true," and cried. She comforted me for a long time while I cried and told her how much it hurt. I later told her some more about the day it happened, about my grandmother's role in covering it up. We also talked about repression of memory and later self-disclosure. The next day my mother related something that she remembered of a time when my father collected my sister and myself after we had spent a day with my grandparents. My grandparents said they had washed and dried my clothes after I had wet myself. In fact, my grandfather washed the blood from my clothes after buggering me. I was crying when I got home and my mother thought it was because I was ashamed of wetting myself and had reassured me that as an accident it was ok.

That weekend my mother and I also did some nice things—shopping and looking at antiques and the local church. Before she went we agreed that neither of us would tell my father, or confront my grandmother, without telling the other. My mother respects the fact that it is my truth to tell as and when I am ready. I gave her some telephone numbers of organizations she could contact and the name of a very good book so that she could understand what damage had been done to me and what I was going through. I think the whole thing has brought us closer together. Before I told her, I felt that my memories were becoming a barrier between us. None of my family could understand my seeming preoccupation with the past, or my need to see a therapist. They couldn't see, as I now understand, why I was quite so angry about the mentally abusive things which my father did in my later childhood and why I must confront him about them at some time.

Yesterday I went sailing for the first time this season and got in touch with a whole load of forgotten muscles. Today, as I write this in my lunch break, they are reminding me of their presence. I am working out my notice before joining a new company and looking forward to a new set of challenges in the future. I also look forward to the day when I can say that yes, I was sexually abused in childhood but I have recovered from its effects and I feel that now I am the person I was always meant to be, but stronger because of my experience.

ANONYMOUS

## Scars

Bulldozer
comes
and lays bare my soil
scraping the sward
of buttercups, sorrel
and knotweed. Did
I ask for this?
Did I see you coming
or you see me?
Was there any need
for this? A swarm
of seagulls
picked my bones bare
from all directions
the seagull hordes
homed in and jumped
squabbled as they
picked. I watched them
in horrid fascination—
sprayed with insecticides
then built upon (know
that feeling of
who the hell am I?) oh

you thought you'd got me made
you thought you could
build fires on my stomach
write your name on my skin.
Let me tell you something:
nature is most rampant
in graveyards:
I've already grown
my own future.

SANDRA BARNES

---

I joined the Survivors' Network in Brighton last year. This was the first organization of its kind that I've ever encountered.

However, they don't seem to keep in touch as often as I'd like, and although I asked to join a self-help group six months ago, they seem to have ignored me.

I think it would be a very good idea if, parallel to the launching of this anthology, a national body of survivors could be set up. This should be an educational, political pressure group. I feel very strongly that survivors must act together as a political force, and this is not happening.

Survivors should forge links with other abused sections of society—working alongside women's refuges, the English Collective of Prostitutes, the Anti-Nazi League and the trade unions, for example.

I am annoyed that many survivors seem to argue that we are a "charitable" rather than a "political" concern. Sometimes I feel we must really take action, not just "amongst ourselves," but in the wider society, too.

This should mean raising awareness in the community—talking in schools and colleges, and especially in the *media*, instead of just running talks for professional "care" workers, as the Brighton group seems to spend more time doing rather than providing a public forum for survivors themselves.

Hell! I'm nineteen years old, and I've done with lying down. I want to make the world realize what it's doing to us. Child sexual abuse is the thorn in my side, and I won't stop complaining until I think I've been given justice.

I really think a national group should be set up, and if no one else is going to do it, then maybe I should. *What do you think?*

KOURTNEY TEMYATIN

---

I am a thirty-two-year-old incest survivor.

I am *also* a musician, a Community Arts worker, an ex-infant teacher, with a BA (honors) and a PGCE. I love writing, painting, sewing, creating and being out in nature, especially near the sea. I am currently studying counselling skills part-time at university. However, most of my time and energy is spent "simply" being a mother to my three-year-old daughter, running the home, and being a partner!

EMMA BENNETT

---

Now for something completely different!

When I've shared my childhood experiences with people, I'm usually asked, "What has stopped you from becoming bitter and twisted?" This is what I reply . . .

There are two things. The first is my sense of humor. In my apartment I have an A5-sized poster that reads: IF YOU SEE SOME-ONE WITHOUT A SMILE—GIVE THEM ONE! It has a big, bright yellow smiley face on it.

I guess that's one of the things I am for—inner happiness. And the second?

I've always known I'm going to make it.

When I'm rich and famous you can say, "I know her, she's my friend." I'm often heard to quote this (or anyone!). When I was very young, I was absolutely convinced that I was an alien sent from another planet (I still think that sometimes)!

Seriously though, I always *knew*, beyond the shadow of a doubt, that I was going to be rich and famous one day. It might take ten or twenty years, but I have this inner core, this absolute conviction, that I *know* I'm going to make it.

So, eternal optimist that I am, this is what keeps the smile on my face and hope in my heart and enables me to bounce back time and again. So keep smiling!

SAM JONES

## The revenge of the doormat

Totally flattened by the door,
We ragged doormats can take no more,
Last-straw time has arrived at last,
Rise up and scream with a loud blast.
The dust may scatter—it may not be nice,
Let's shake off the shackles and eradicate the lice.
It sounds like you want to rebel,
But how long can you stay quiet in this living hell?
Life's too short to be treated like that,
Say your piece—don't stay a doormat.

MARY-GRACE

CHARACTERS WHO USED TO INTIMIDATE ME:
MY PERSONNEL OFFICER AT WORK AND MY FATHER

# I picture her . . .

I picture her
The sweetest sight
The strongest,
Most vivid image.

She cycles around
The streets of Manchester.
With locks as strong as the chains
That bind us.

Free
Loose
Open to
The wind
The rain
And the Goddesses of Sun and Moon.
Elements in unison
Play joyful games
They are with her.

She claims back
The day by night
The night by day.
These streets she reclaims
Are for all her Black Sisters.

She cleanses them
Of those bitter,
Bad-tasting memories
Of abusers in corners.
Of colluding communities
Whose silence
Attempted
To hold her tongue.

But now you are back
With your hand in hers
And my voice
Is as soft as her face
As strong as her locks
And I am shouting proud
And I am reclaiming
Those streets of those
Small towns in big cities;

Chorlton cum Hardy
Whalley Range
Longsight
Moss side
Shelthorpe
Thorpe Hill
Melton Road
Highfields
Camden
Battersea
Deptford

These cities,
These towns.

Those places,
Those times.

I claim them back
I make them mine.

RAMANI

JANINE GUICE

## You ask me why it is I cry?

People say hush now—there, there
To stop the tears from flowing.
Yet all they succeed in doing,
Is stopping me from growing.

Tears offer freedom from frustration,
Like a caged-up bird released.
Aggression is my war within
Which tears can make at peace.

Treasure your human emotions,
They are very much deserved.
When you laugh—laugh loud!
And when you cry be proud.

MARY HELEN TREASURER

## An exciting, exhilarating, extraordinary event

At 1.30 p.m. on Saturday, 11 September 1993, numerous banners, billowing and bobbing like the sails of a great fleet, launched into Park Lane from Hyde Park on a sea of purple ribbons.

It wasn't a dream—it actually happened. An historic, barrier-crashing event took place. Hundreds of children, women and men with a broad diversity of race, culture and sexuality came together to participate in the first national march against child sexual abuse in Britain.

The view from the rear end of the march was truly spectacular. Traffic was blocked off by the police and the procession stretched out ahead as far as the eye could see. I really felt the impact of the occasion when the front of the march could be seen in the distance curving to the right on the approach to Hyde Park Corner.

So many people! Individuals and groups of female and male survivors, mothers' groups, partners, children, parents, friends, workers, supporters and a quintet of saxophonists brought shoppers, tourists and hotel staff to a standstill. Many looked stunned and thoughtful as they read the banners and realized the purpose of the march. Others applauded. Some joined the march, which one of the police said he had never seen happen before. Onlookers packed the pavements in Piccadilly, around Eros and in the Haymarket before the march reached its destination of Trafalgar Square.

All the banners were displayed on the steps behind the platform in Trafalgar Square flanked by the sculptures of majestic lions. Without doubt, the setting was perfect and symbolic. The strength of the lions was mirrored and outshone by the scores of survivors, mothers and partners who took the platform, one by one, to speak out courageously against child sexual abuse.

A male survivor spoke, seated in his wheelchair, to highlight the need to recognize the huge numbers of people with disabilities and/or learning difficulties who are abused.

A Muslim woman and an African woman pleaded for the issue to be addressed by everyone from all cultures and races.

One mother told us that she would leave the rally to collect her daughter from an access visit to her father which she was bound by a judge to comply with. On each occasion she collected her daughter hoping for one of two things. Either her ex-partner would not have abused the child that day or he would have abused her to the degree that sufficient evidence would be available to prevent further visits.

A number of survivors of ritual abuse shared some of their feelings and emphasized the necessity to believe in the existence of ritual abuse.

At regular intervals, between individuals speaking, two women sang songs they had composed. Another young woman, with a backing group created on the day, gave a rousing rendition of the disco hit "I will survive."

Poignant poetry, meaningful music, wonderful words, thousands of tears and lots of laughs were generously shared in an electric atmosphere of acceptance. Something which had been denied to so many of the people there for so long.

Sue Melrose, who instigated and co-ordinated the march, resolutely refused to take any credit for the day. She insisted that the day, and its success, belonged equally to everyone present and to all victims and survivors unable to be there. In her short opening address she asked for those survivors who felt able to raise their hands. The majority of people did so. She then asked for raised hands from everyone who knew another survivor who couldn't be there. Who knew five more? Who knew ten more? Who knew twenty? Who knew a hundred?

Under the watchful eye of Nelson, atop his column, another battle had been fought and won. A public display of unity amongst diverse groups of survivors and supporters, assembled together, must render obsolete the denial of the extent of child sexual abuse. It also pours shame on the deafening silence of the national press. Except by *Company* magazine and *The Big Issue*, the march was not considered newsworthy. Nevertheless, the entire event was filmed by BBC2 and will be included in two programs of *First Sight* in October. The national press may then realize they missed something very special.

The march and rally illustrated how crucial the empowerment of survivors is as a vital element of the war to combat CSA. Summit has written beautifully and strongly of the need for a survivors' revolt. Sue Melrose was inspired to instigate the march and form CROSS— Campaign for Rights Of Survivors of Sexual abuse—after attending the survivors' discussion day organized by Beverley Ledgard of Harrow Survivors' Group in March 1993.

On that day, Sue was prompted to speak of the court action she had recently lost against her parents. She spoke of the need to change the Limitation Act which prevents civil legal actions by survivors six years after the last incident of abuse, or their eighteenth birthday. As so many survivors repress their memories of the abuse, this is clearly an inappropriate and unjust Act. Someone at the discussion day suggested delivering a petition to Downing Street and the rest, as they say, is history.

The success of the march owes much to the strength of Sue Melrose's ability and genuine wish to consider, listen to and accommodate the views and help of everyone who wanted to be involved.

Future events will rely on the nurture of the belief that each of us has the power to make a difference. The meeting place for this year's march was the Reform Tree in Hyde Park which is actually now a lamp-post in the middle of a large circle of tarmac. Hopefully, next year's will require the whole of Hyde Park.

SEE YOU THERE!

Ros Barber

We should not make a way of life out of surviving. If we see ourselves as nothing but survivors we are still being defined by the abusive relationship and so by the abuser. So we must, if we can, move on to become our full and separate selves.

LIZ

Well here I am and I'm proud of it! It's felt like a long struggle, and at times it still is, but I guess I've survived and whatever happens next I can keep going. I feel like I've achieved a lot in my life and I'm slowly learning to listen to what I want, rather than conforming to an oppressive society. It feels good to realize I can make choices about every aspect of myself and that I deserve to be happy.

I have found healing a painful, devastating, alive and enriching experience. At the moment I feel furious with my parents for abusing me, but I feel proud that I have proved that I no longer need them and have started to break free from the messages they gave me. I am my own person now.

For me, the most important part of healing has been reaching out and asking others for support and connecting with other survivors. For anyone reading this I'd like to say: you don't have to be alone—there are people out there who can help and it is brave to ask for what you need. Hang on, for gradually the pain will become less intense. This may be so slow that you don't even realize it's happening, but it will be. I believe we can all make it through and survive, and we all deserve a great big party one day to celebrate!

PENNY K.

I still have a long way to go in relation to my healing because it involves so much more than the sexual abuse, but at the moment I feel stronger than I have felt in a long time, and I also feel in a position where I want and feel able to help other people who have experienced abuse.

PENNY

---

For thirty years I have been in and out of mental hospitals. In between I have loved life, read, and been creative.

My sons are my treasure and thrill in my life. I divorced years ago.

I am recently on Lithium and for two or three years I have been attending Saifline in Plymouth. It helps me greatly. We are such friends and endeavor to be supportive and have ideas for each other.

At the age of fifty-two my abuse and illness are part of my life. Part of me. However, I have a dogged perseverance so I get up each time.

I love reading. I now write, and I'm into general knowledge. I'm good with my hands. I also work on my family tree and am interested in art, the West Country, railways, Russia, knitting, politics—and epitaphs. Mine is

**1941–?**
**Roberta Grace**
**Who ran out of**
**fight.**

I am treated so badly by the community in general so I treat myself lovingly.

ROBERTA ST. CLAIRE

---

And now . . .

I admire and praise myself for my strength, my courage, my tenacity, my integrity, my expertise, my knowledge, my intelligence, in fact everything that I am.

One of the most difficult things for me to bring out into the world is my softness, my gentleness, my beauty and my love for bright-colored, long and softly flowing clothes. I still practice wearing them at home or in other safe places first and of course I choose when and where to let that part of me shine through.

I've used my own healing to change my career. I left school and trained as a hairdresser. When I gave that up I worked in various factories feeding myself into the zombie, fodder, walking dead society. That was nine years ago. Since then I have written, directed and performed my own play about incest called *Breaking the Silence*. I have worked with Extemporary Dance and performed with other women in "Women on the Move," where we performed our own stories in dance.

I worked with a core group of women running various arts workshops (with absolutely no experience, only an ocean of enthusiasm!) for a few months. This culminated in an exhibition "For Women by Women." It was tremendously exciting to see the wealth and the high standard of work we produced in the form of poetry, sculpture, photography, masks, etc., when many of us had never done anything like it before.

I choose as much as I dare at present about my whole life. I write, I sing, I dance, I play music in celebration of my beautiful inner child and my beautiful outer woman. I celebrate life as life celebrates me.

Not bad going for someone who suffered abuse and torture from birth to fifteen years of age. Incredible for a heroin, morphine, cocaine, Ritalin etc., etc., addict of thirteen years' standing.

All due to the little, blue-eyed daydreamer of a girl who held on to this: "You don't know me and you never will. But I'll tell you something—you'll never stop me. One day I'm going to write a book about all this and there's nothing you can do about it."

B.W.W.

# A poem to my father

Look here, at me, your daughter!
A subject of your derision and falsehood . . .
You can be proud!
Pious fraud that is you . . .
The litany, the lip-service, the lies,
The attrition, the fantasy, the disdain.
These things are yours.
But you couldn't take me all
You couldn't grasp at my light
You couldn't grope at my color
The ocher, the sienna; the liberty,
The will, the spirit, the poetry.
These things have *always* been mine!
Unpolluted by the filth that is yours.
You! The grotesque incarnate,
Your masked obscenity marbled through that sickness
You're a suffusion of your own disease,
These things are you
But you couldn't take me all . . .
For with each Solstice Sun I understand,
So each symbolic death . . . brings a rebirth
Its endurance an expression of my own survival.
I couldn't grow in that knowledge you gave me,
And your destruction of me can teach you nothing!
So . . . as you bathe in your fear and pathos,
I will honor the beauty of rebirth . . . the Solstice Sun
The Solstice Sun . . . a time of beginnings and a time of
    endings.
Because you *didn't* take me all!

ANGIE MORTIMER-FARTHING

# Oh me

Little me and big me
old me and new me
First me and every me
Changing me
Rearranging me.

Real me and false me
Accepting me
The whole of me
Truly me
Wonderful me.

MARY J. McMAHON

---

I am now culling my past. Pain, grief, anger and self-effacement will become superimposed on a feeling of being in control of my existence. Ghosts that still try to pull me down and impose a pulsating despair on the depths of my nights, or after fleeting recognition of the stuff my loneliness has been made of, will be firmly and politely asked to leave. With increasing clarity and strength I shall be able to see myself as the giant that I am, holding a barely transparent dove's egg in my hand; within that egg are members of my family, bound, unable to see out of the little shell, unable even to want to break out. My process of enormous growth has begun. Forty-seven years of my victimhood will be sent to the archives, and a refurbished model of me created. I will no longer weep for the old times; new times will be born, and there will be rejoicing by soul-giants on both sides of eternity. Anger and pain will become merely a couple of words in a dictionary that is full of them. The counselor that will help me will emerge from I know not where, I know not when. She will be one that can see beyond duality, and may arrive only when I am at the point of leaving. I suspect she has already arrived. For the moment, I give myself permission to grieve, to reflect, to write for a book. Beyond pain, beyond anger, there is a wisdom and a strength that I've gained the merest glimpse of.

OLGA CHEN

## Oranges

Going down again,
(Not for the third time,
I passed that long ago)
I chance upon the finality
Of non-feeling.
Of endless, changeless, timelessness,
Of death by non-being
And silent denial,
Of infinite choicelessness,
Of cryogenic pain
Gone but not forgotten,
Senseless, easeless.
Gnawing at my bones
Fossilized in perpetuity.
Touching no one.

And I see golden oranges
Glowing in the sunlight
I hear winds surging, urging,
The heart-breaking of waves
Against the patient rock,
Sense diamond raindrops purifying
As they go dancing by,
Watch the child-like dolphin
Ever ready for life
And know at last that I
Must take my part
In this living turmoil,
Lest I deny myself

The blessing of life's fingers
Open and outstretched.
In touch with life.

CARO

## Choices

Choices are like a tree that goes all through my life. Beginning with
that all-purpose single center, then branching and changing and
branching again through twigs and tangles to its utmost tips. I wouldn't
say I've always chosen where I was going, or what I would be, but at
every branching I have made a choice of some sort, and that has led to
the next choice. There is a form and pattern that my tree follows,
reaching out all the time. I've always thought of it as the hawthorn,
blasted by the wind, gnarled, clinging to a rock. Grey twigs bent this
way and that, surviving through everything. Sometimes though I am
something far more tender, succulent, flowing and uncluttered. A wil-
low tree perhaps or maybe the mountain ash. Yes, I like that, a survivor,
but its limbs are straighter and it has bright red buttons in the autumn.

JULIE COCKBURN

## On dancing

I've never been one for formal dancing.

But my mother danced around the house like some great and
beautiful goddess, so I copied her from the age of five.

In front of the mirror on my own with bangles over my ears and
a towel for a shawl.

Very glam.

This went on for twenty years or so.

My friends and I frequented the dance floors at least twice a
week for ten years or more.

Some of my friends picked up men, or vice versa.

I preferred to give vent to my anger by weaving slow and snaky around the music or stomping, flicking and punching to the rhythm. Those men who thought they'd have half a chance, I either out-danced or merrily flicked off my very strong hips with one foul sweep so that they landed splat on the floor.

Wonderful.

and I still cherish this taste of shamanism, dancing.

JANINE GUICE

## True flight

Fear you all . . . that little girl
The one that never died
A fragment of her former self
Amid that black decay

Confusing cliffs of rock all round
The comforting sky way above her
She must learn the true nature of flight
"CLIP" Her wings and soar

For *Them* it's not over—it is not finished
For she is alive and will fly
Her courage will lead where she must go
Long have *They* feared this end to *Their* Saga

JAN CHAPPLE (NÉE DURKIN)

---

And I survived, didn't I?
I can go to the grave without feeling shame or guilt;
I can sleep soundly in my bed;
I can face God with a clean conscience;
and maybe, just maybe, I can even help
other five-year-olds who are just like I was—

riddled with guilt and shame and living in a state of constant
terror.

Trying to escape from the Death Camp
they call Home.

                                            ANONYMOUS

---

My first memories were triggered by being in a relationship with a
sexually addicted man. Oh no, so my family really was as bad as all
those other ones, the ones that the upper classes turn their noses up
at. How could I possibly confront all this in myself and my family?
But I did and still am all the time . . .

I have been healing from my sexual abuse and dysfunctional
childhood for nearly eight years now, and having written this I feel
really amazing. I *am* really amazing.

I feel very, very powerful and very successful and that I certainly have something to say to everyone, but particularly to those
who have been sexually abused and abandoned in upper-class families.

                                            HARRIET

---

Yes—i'm all right
i'm sorry i bothered you.
No—i'm not all right
and still sorry i bothered you.

I'm alone—
feeling hemmed in
trying to explain that God is good
to someone else.
He didn't let it happen.
Man's free will did that

But God does demand that
        we forgive

We are to forgive
                the stolen childhood
                the innocence lost
                the pain inflicted
We are to forgive
                the abuse of our bodies
                    of our souls

—and in the midst of forgiveness
        try to heal ourselves
    so we can become real
                    not shadow women
    driven by the fear
                of inadequacy
                of guilt
  for what was done
                not deserved
                not asked for
  inflicted on our   young
                clean
                unsullied
                  minds

We are to forgive
                emotions not understood
                love expressed
        so ours is suppressed.

Yet in spite of this
           we grew
           we married
                  had children
                  divorced
                  lived alone

We sometimes lost faith
in God and ourselves
We doubted the goodness
inherent in man and woman
We respond eagerly to the kind word
while examining what it means

And still we need to forgive him
                and
                    ourselves!!

FRANCES GRANT

---

Ha fear
I know you too well
I am love
and more powerful than you
you can fight all you like
but I have no need to battle
I flow peacefully
So why not accept the fact
that I'm wise to your act
It's a losing battle can't you see
I'll always overcome you
      disperse you
I'll never tire of loving you see
for I am endless
Universal
Cosmic

MAURA RYAN

## A survivors' checklist

Could any of these statements describe you?

- You know what others are thinking or feeling without them uttering a word.
- You have a special affinity with pets, especially cats.
- You clean your house from top to bottom every day, put everything neatly in its right place and feel very anxious if anyone messes it up.
- You have a teddy that you clutch at times of stress.
- You have the ability to work or study or both while inside you feel as though the world is "falling apart."
- You can find joy in the tiniest flower, the faintest rainbow.
- You are constantly on the lookout for what might go wrong—never quite believing that you will be ok.
- You take great care not to be too much of a burden to others.
- You give much more than you dare accept.
- You strive to please and keep people happy.
- You are always convinced it *must* be *your* turn to pay for tea, drinks, cakes, etc.

If one or more of these describes you—Congratulations!
    You just *might* be a survivor!

LINDA FARTHING